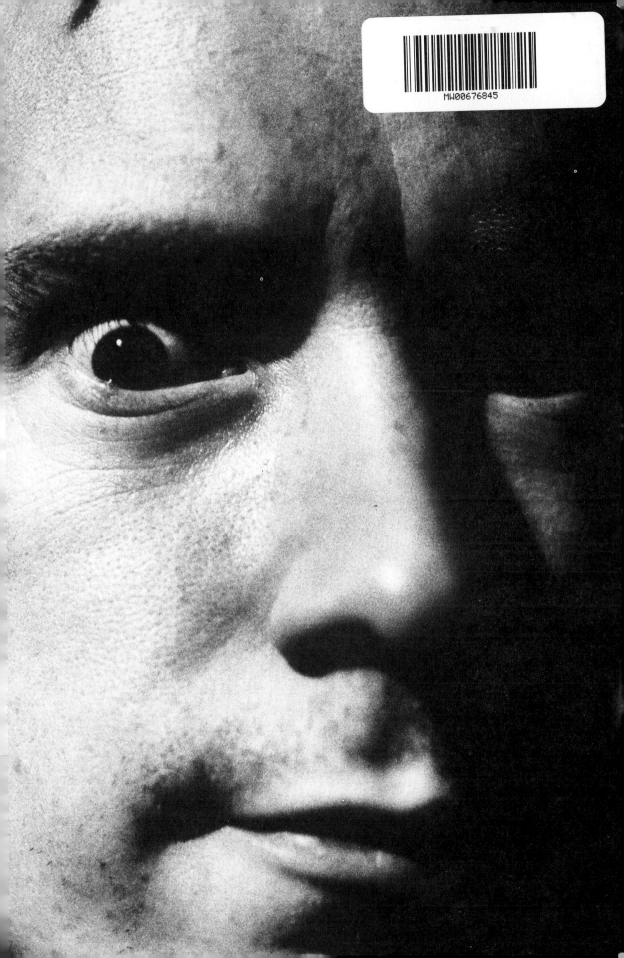

RiSE/FALL

PUBLiC iMAGE LiMiTED

clinton heylin

Edited by Chris Charlesworth
Book Designed by Ranch Associates
Picture Research by Debbie Dorman
Project and typesetting co-ordinated by Caroline Watson

ISBN 0.7119.1684.5
Order No: OP45012

Exclusive distributors:

Book Sales Limited,
8/9 Frith Street,
London W1V 5TZ, UK.

Music Sales Corporation,
225 Park Avenue South,
New York, NY 10003, USA.

Music Sales Pty Limited,
120 Rothschild Avenue,
Rosebery, NSW 2018, Australia.

To the Music Trade only:
Music Sales Limited,
8/9 Frith Street,
London W1V 5TZ, UK.

Picture credits:
Peter Anderson, p1, 6, 9, 18, Edrei Communications Corp, p42, Kevin
Cummins, p27, London Features Int, Front Cover, p15, 21, 23, 28/29, 37,
38, 41, 46, 49, 56/57, 59, 60, 64, 66, 69, 71, 72, 74, 77, 80, 83, 85, 87, 96,
Melody Maker, p51, Dennis Morris, p2/3, Pictorial Press, p32, 34, 78,
Marcia Resnick, p44/45, Kate Simon, p4, 24, 52, Jo Stevens, p17,
Virgin Records, p31, Warner/Reprise, p12.

Every effort has been made to trace the copyright holders of the
photographs in this book but one or two were unreachable. We would be
grateful if the photographers concerned would contact us.

Typeset by Capital Setters, London.
Printed in England by Anchor Press Ltd, Tiptree, Essex.

Omnibus Press
London · New York · Sydney · Cologne

This is the story of Public Image Limited, from audacious experimental combo to The Johnny Rotten Cabaret Show. It is also the story of 'the public image', for the story of PiL is as much about the way that PiL were perceived by the media (the UK music press in particular), as the activities of its personnel.

More than anything 'Rise/Fall' is a reminder of routes PiL have laid out for others to follow, hopefully sending the reader back to the music, the power and the glory, that was PiL. The cassette plays poptones . . .

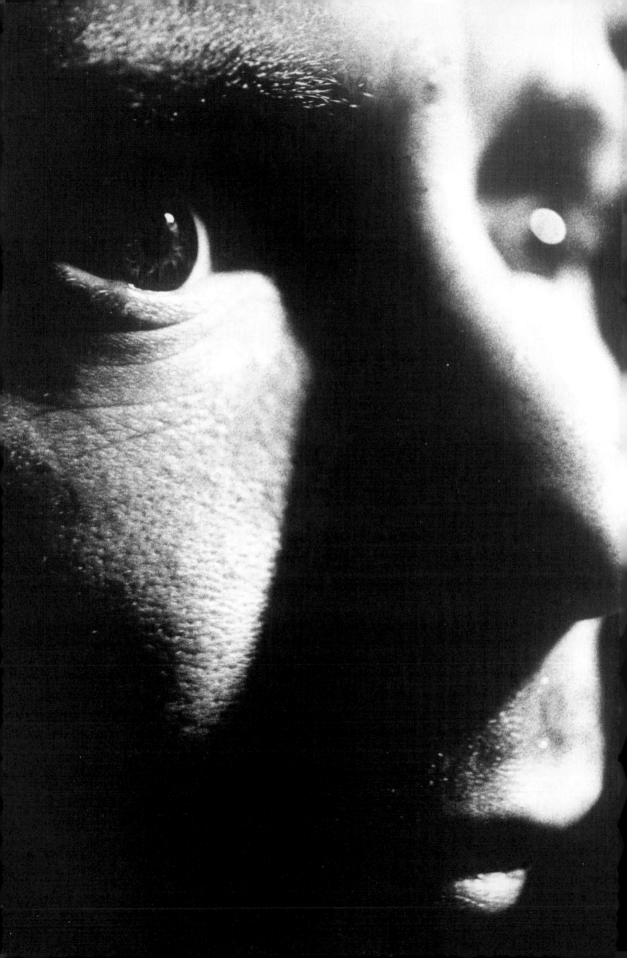

CHAPTER 1

'Lonely musician seeks comfort in fellow trendies'

"Rock (music) is an example of a youth cult that became mass culture over time: pest became host. Punk is an example, like Dada, of a pesky youth cult that threatened to replace the host culture . . . Whether observers are partisan to pest or host, the interest is in that attacking moment when all risks are poised to leap. Such moments lurk in the history of every movement and the clock never stands still. But to leap is to exchange fluidity for power, inspiration for dogma, and insight for wisdom. Pest becoming host, success becomes hollow: 'There's no success like failure.' Alternatively, when the youth cult leaps and fails, there is no second chance. Instead, threat turns to whimper and predatory forces digest it: 'Failure is no success at all.' *Dadapunk* by W.T. Lhamon.

It was ironic that the English punk movement should take its name from a motley collection of US garage-bands from the late sixties who rebelled against the rise of West Coast music and drew their inspiration from the British Invasion bands of 1964/5; ironic because commercial success for these garage-bands was ephemeral. Their finest hour-and-a-half can be heard on a classic compilation LP entitled 'Nuggets', which succinctly captures each band's 'moment', a magical, transitory, fleeting footnote in the history of pop music.

Likewise the English punk movement, though vastly more important than its American predecessor, had an inbuilt self-destruct button, as Pete Townshend observed in 'Won't Get Fooled Again' – 'Meet the new boss/ Same as the old boss.'

Indeed, as Lhamon has suggested above, the choices were twofold: internal combustion or inevitable dilution. With the possible exception of Elvis Costello (who was really more of a latecomer from the brief pub-rock boom with his r'n'b combo Flip City), none of the important artists who emerged in 1976 and 1977 ever improved on their first records. In the case of The Sex Pistols the band had already arranged its own demise with the sacking of Glen Matlock in March 1977; whilst the other 'leaders' The Clash, always professing a desire to overthrow The Rolling Stones, duly became a parody of their mentors.

If punk was modern music's version of Dadaism ("a short lived movement in art which sought to abandon all form and throw off all tradition") then its second wave (in 1978) – generally known as New Wave or New Music – was music's version of Surrealism. For their approach to music was far more self-consciously 'arty' (and a lot less nihilistic) than previous punk incarnations.

Inevitably the leading lights of the New Wave were those musicians from the punk movement who thought things through and realised that the negative elements of the punk message could easily decline into nihilism. In the case of Howard Devoto (with Magazine) and John Lydon (with PiL) they had to wholly abandon the pop sensibilities of their punk bands (Buzzcocks and The Sex Pistols) and start again. In the case of Siouxsie of The Banshees and the members of Warsaw (soon to become Joy Division and then New Order), the bands managed to mature before recording their first albums and emerge relatively untainted by any of their primordial punk origins.

In Siouxsie's case her improvisation of 'The Lord's Prayer' at the September 1976 100 Club Punk Festival was the ultimate expression of a Dadaist approach to music; though the stark, metallic sound that The Banshees developed over the next 18 months was never mainstream enough to be called punk by anyone save the most deluded of observers.

In Lydon's case there was never any question that a new music could be created within the confines of The Pistols. Whether he consciously realised it or not, The Sex Pistols were there to bring to an end the history of rock 'n' roll, by blowing these embossed images of stardom up in everybody's face. Their famous final epitaph: "Ha Ha Ha Ever get the feeling you've been cheated. G'night," was intended to complete the act of destruction.

Of course one possibility open to Lydon after The Pistols' demise would have been a sanctimonious exhumation of the corpse of rock music which would have flattered the fans and provided his pension. Clearly though, throughout his days in New York at the end of January 1978 and

Jamaica through February such a notion does not appear to have seriously crossed his mind, though on his return from Jamaica he was apparently telling anyone who would listen: "I've decided to become a parody of myself, because it's amusing. I'm looking forward to having six kids, a home in the country, a wonderful mortgage, ever so middle-class. And a Rolls-Royce – vintage of course. And a villa on the Isle of Wight. P.S. I am now living with Norman Wisdom."

Instead Lydon galvanised himself into a frenetic enough bout of activity to recruit an entire band, write half a dozen songs with them and start sculpting a new sound – all this by the middle of May 1978 and despite initial auditions in March not being particularly fruitful:

"I went through weeks and weeks of rehearsing with everybody who bothered to reply to my ad in the music press. It said something like 'Lonely musician seeks comfort in fellow trendies . . .' I didn't use my own name because then people who didn't know how to play would have turned up and that would have set me back another two years. But the people who did turn up were terrible. Denim clad heavy metal fans.

"So eventually I thought 'Ah! Wobble! He can play – vaguely!' So I rang him up. And Keith (Levene) rang up the next night. I'd been looking for him ever since I started to form the new band but he wasn't on the phone. And then Jim (Walker) was the only person I liked from the auditions. He's amazing. He sounds like Can's drummer. All double beats."

Lydon's antecedents to this point have been fairly well documented, but what of the others? Only Levene had any kind of pedigree in music. Having apparently received classical training in both guitar and piano 'well into his teens', Levene was also a member of The Clash for their first half-dozen gigs, including a 'support-slot' at The Roundhouse at the beginning of September 1976 – probably his last gig with the band. Levene put his departure down to band politics, the other members of the band to his penchant for illegal substances.

Whatever the case, Levene then became part of

Siouxsie

the short-lived Flowers Of Romance which also featured assorted future members of The Sex Pistols (Sid Vicious) and The Slits (Palm Olive and Viv Albertine) for whom he also worked as a sound engineer.

Jim Walker, a 23-year old Canadian from Vancouver, apparently came over to Britain after hearing the wave of exciting music coming from the land of Albion. Jah Wobble, like Levene, was an old friend of Lydon's who first met him at Kingsway College of Further Education in 1971. He was not initially impressed: "I thought he was a Led Zeppelin fan. I was queueing up behind him and we had a bit of a quarrel about who was going to put their name down first . . . After that he just started crawling around after me, and I let him be my mate. He used to have to buy me drinks though, 'cos no one liked him then."

Caroline Coon

As early as mid-May, when *NME*'s Neil Spencer became the first to interview the new as-yet-unnamed combo, the band had worked up at least two original songs into playable form: 'Religion' (aka 'Sod In Heaven') and 'Public Image'. The words for 'Religion' were written by John while he was still in The Pistols. They also worked on two songs from The Pistols' repertoire, 'EMI' and 'Belsen Was A Gas', plus a song Wobble introduced as, "A vision I had last night," it turned out to be The Who's 'My Generation'.

According to Neil Spencer the sound he heard at the rehearsal . . . "at times sounded more like something from 'Electric Ladyland' than your archetypal three-chord punk powerthrash." Though the band sounded nothing like The Pistols, Wobble was quick to deny they were a reggae band either: "Rock is obsolete. But it's our music, our basic culture. People thought we were gonna play reggae, but we ain't gonna be no GT Moore and The Reggae Guitars or nothing. It's just a natural influence – like I play heavy on the bass."

One other journalist who managed to hear the band in its embryonic stage was Caroline Coon, who like Spencer had known Lydon during his time with The Pistols. Her article in a July edition of *Sounds* was entitled 'Public Image'. Despite Coon's hint the band remained unnamed, though various joke titles had been under never-too-serious discussion: 'The Carnivorous Buttockflies', 'The Future Features', 'The Windsor Up-Lift' and 'The Royal Family'.

Asked to describe his new sound, Lydon told Coon it was, "Total pop with deep meanings." However Coon's opinion of the band's progress was not quite so flattering as Spencer's had been: "Ideally he'd like to start gigging in six weeks time. On the evidence of rehearsals I've heard however, that seems somewhat optimistic. With hard work and luck, the band could be ready in six months. Recording is another matter . . ."

It certainly was. By the following week the band were on the front cover of *Melody Maker* christened 'Public Image' (though not as yet Limited), and were ensconced in the first of several studios recording their début single 'Public Image' (supposedly due for release on September 8). It was here that they really started to create a sound together.

They also began work on their début album. Unfortunately they developed a habit of getting banned from studios at a rate closely proximate with the rate The Pistols used to be banned from concert venues. Among studios where recordings came to an abrupt halt were Advision and Wessex Studios (the latter had been used by The Pistols when EMI were paying the bills).

According to a report in *Sounds* the ban at Wessex followed "an altercation with an engineer . . . After the dialogue got a little heated, the engineer rather mysteriously launched his head at a bottle which, not unnaturally, broke."

Meanwhile, with the single 'Public Image' in the can, the band found they had to address themselves to the question of marketing themselves. A major part of The Sex Pistols' success had been down to the shrewd use of Jamie Reid's remarkable ideas for logos and adverts, all bound to a common image and theme. Public Image now needed to present themselves as something different, but equally important. The first requirement was a logo, the now well-known PiL logo, a pill-like design with a black strip down the middle and the letters P-i-L in black, white and black. The logo was introduced in initial adverts for the single.

In fact these adverts simply consisted of the logo, with 'A product of your society' written below, and the terse note at the bottom of the page: 'Public Image Ltd – The Band – The Public Image – The Single'. The single itself was wrapped in a mock newspaper, which included one of three further ads, each featuring a different member of the band. In Lydon's, John asked, "How come you're such a hit with the girls Keith?" Levene answered (in his ad), "I discovered PiL." Wobble played on his reputation as something of a hardnut with, "I was wild with my chopper until I discovered PiL."

The mock newspaper sleeve also included part of the *NME* report about the band's failure to appear on ITV's pop show, *Revolver* the previous month. The article was entitled, 'Refused to play Russian Roulette'.

They were due to appear on the programme in September to promote their forthcoming single but only Levene turned up, accompanied by a Virgin lackey. The other three had absconded to Camber Sands. Producer Mickie Most sat and waited, fuming all the while. Most finally retorted, "I think he (Lydon)'s done himself a lot of harm, as breaking your contract like that means an instant life ban on independent television. He's bound to need a television plug sometime in the next 20 years and he won't be able to get it."

According to Lydon: "We had previously arranged that an entire programme of *Revolver* would be in our control, we would produce it totally, decide what bands would be on it plus we would be in it at some point. We set it up and then Virgin in 'our best interests' decided to ring the *Revolver* people up and ask, 'Was it at all possible that we do ONE song on the programme?' So *Revolver* immediately cancelled what we'd arranged."

In fact Most's ban lasted an impressive three weeks, since the video of 'Public Image' (filmed in September) was featured on London Weekend Television's *Saturday Night People* on October 21, drawing the extensive review 'Repulsive' from self-styled mordant wit Clive James. This was in fact the band's only TV appearance to promote their first single, issued on October 13, though it still reached number nine in the singles charts, buoyed by several favourable reviews (including a mightily enthusiastic one from Giovanni Dadomo in *Sounds*: "It will be a massive hit, and deserves to be"). Indeed end of the year lists for 'Best Singles Of 1978' by *Melody Maker*, *NME* and *Sounds* placed the single first, second and second respectively (losing out in the latter two polls to the Buzzcocks' 'Ever Fallen In Love' and Patti Smith's 'Because The Night').

The song also afforded fans their first opportunity to hear the new band and assess its potential. As such Public Image, though it featured Wobble's rumbling bass, Lydon's nasal whine and Levene's ringing, metallic guitar, gave a slightly distorted picture, presenting the illusion of a pop group – albeit one with a most unusual sound. Such assessments proved premature.

What the single did provide PiL with was a public for their image, while clearly placing them well outside any pseudo-Pistols niche in which others may have been looking to place Lydon. As such the single was a most successful culmination to half a year's trading. For with the release of the single, 'Public Image' the band became a company – PUBLIC IMAGE LIMITED.

CHAPTER 2

*'You should have seen Branson's face
when he heard that . . . he was furious'*

While the single received its plaudits and moved up the charts, the band were hard at work on their début album. Given that PiL had existed barely six months it is not surprising they had insufficient material for a full album, but they wanted further product released by the end of the year.

This was made all the more important when it was announced at the beginning of October that PiL would make their official UK live début at The Rainbow Theatre in London's Finsbury Park on Christmas Day and play a second show on Boxing Day. There had initially been concern that the GLC might not give the go-ahead for the show because of Lydon's past associations, but these fears proved unfounded.

PiL's début album was scheduled for release on December 8, a time when album sales in general would be at their pre-Christmas height. To illustrate the fact that the band were working on the album right up to the last minute, the front cover listed only five tracks because the other two songs ('Attack' and 'Fodderstompf') remained unrecorded when the front cover was designed.

The problem of finding studios willing to accommodate PiL hadn't helped the progress of the recording. Lydon commented on some of the difficulties when asked by Chris Salewicz in December 1978 where the album was actually recorded:

"All over the place. The Manor (in Oxon), the new Virgin London studio at Shepherd's Bush, a reggae studio in Wardour Street. We used nearly every studio there is. We ran out of them in the end. They're all so-o-o-o bad. They all cater for MOR sounds. If you want anything out of the ordinary out of the desks it gets really difficult. To get the sound that's on that album is so hard in those places.

"You have to go through so much bullshit. And all it is, is trying to get a live sound – the way any band should sound on stage . . . you've always got shithead engineers who won't show you the ins and outs of things and who scream blue murder when you turn anything up full."

Of the songs on the album, now christened 'First Issue', it was 'Fodderstompf' which would come in for the most critical flak. Lydon told Salewicz, "You should've seen Branson's face when he heard that . . . he was furious." The song, a seven-and-a-half-minute exercise in 'disco dub', was seen as a desperate attempt to stretch the album to a reasonable length. If 'Fodderstompf' is discounted the album would only clock in at half an hour.

The other problem with the album was its slightly schizophrenic nature, which almost guaranteed an unfavourable critical reception. 'First Issue' was neatly divided between a trilogy of catchy 'singles material' ('Public Image', 'Attack' and 'Low Life') and a trio of lengthier excursions whose emphasis was on sledge-hammer power and a much greater sense of improvisation. Particularly disorienting was the album's opening track 'Theme', a nine-minute (largely improvised) excursion into what it feels like when, "it's dawn on a wet Wednesday in Chelsea and Britain's most powerful punk singer . . . is feeling like death." Indeed of all the tracks Lydon seemed most happy with 'Theme':

"We did that about four or five in the morning. We'd already done a couple of takes but the machine was wrong. Really irritating. I think it sounds great. It's like there's a barrage of guitars all over the place but it's just Keith's one guitar. He's amazing – the racket he can get out of that thing! He's got all the madness that The Pistols had at the start."

It was this major discrepancy in direction that most reviewers seized upon when the album was released that first week in December. Pete Silverton's review in Sounds was perhaps the most unpleasant (and misguided): "A producer friend said it sounded like a band (who had) gone into the studio for the first time and run riot with all the effects." Nick Kent's NME review seized on the three catchy, three-minute dittys as being, "musical territory that, given time and effort, will provide them with a strong and individual foundation for future focus and experimentation." He must have been mighty disappointed with their future direction for it was songs like 'Theme' which provided the best indication of future PiL music.

Just about all the reviews considered the album self-indulgent rather than experimental, and many voiced the (oft-repeated) concern that PiL was in fact an elaborate joke from Lydon, his own version of Lou Reed's 'Metal Machine Music'. Levene: "They all slagged it (the first album) because it was self-indulgent, non-simplistic and non-rock 'n' roll. Those are all good points. But that's the kind of music we intend to make."

At least one reviewer even concluded that Lydon was trying to lose his audience, that the album was deliberately anti-commercial: "Johnny Rotten is going to lose quite a few fans with this record, but as that seems to have been the purpose of it anyway, perhaps the album can be called a success."

Despite all this critical flak the album reached 22 in the charts and still managed to appear at number 28 in *NME*'s 'Best Albums Of 1978'. The album did garner at least one enthusiastic review by Kris Needs in *Zigzag*: "PiL have already got their own sound and this album has moments as biting as any Pistols song. No resting on laurels. No waste."

It was Needs who obtained one of the best interviews from PiL when they gave a series of promotional interviews for both album and single in November 1978. Needless to say Lydon did most of the talking, though he was anxious to emphasise the group-concept:

"In this band we are all equal. No Rod Stewarts. We all do equal amounts of work, we all produce equally, write songs and collect the money equally ... We're just the beginning of a huge umbrella, we can each do our own solo ventures to our own amusement so long as they don't infringe on the band as a whole. I want it to spread out. I know that might sound a bit idealistic ... "

Two such solo ventures were launched at this stage in PiL's development, Jah Wobble's exercise in dub, 'Dreadlock Don't Deal With Wedlock', and a 12-inch EP called 'Steel Leg Versus The Electric Dread' which featured Keith Levene (as 'Stratetime Keith') Jah Wobble, and the resident guest at PiL HQ (Lydon's house) Don Letts, who contributed vocals on one track, 'Haile Unlikely', and subsequently joined The Clash's Mick Jones in Big Audio Dynamite. Wobble and Levene's interests in experimenting with mix, indeed the whole sound, of a song was exemplified here with an instrumental dub version of 'Haile Unlikely' and a further 'exercise in sound', 'Stratetime And The Wide Man'.

More importantly the band made their live début with four shows in December. The first two were in Brussels and Paris and were arranged primarily as warm-ups for the dates at The Rainbow. In fact the first gig in Brussels did not go too well and the band simply played the six songs from the album (minus 'Fodderstompf') and did not return for an encore.

The Paris show was much more successful. The sound was fine and the crowd responded enthusiastically. In fact, as with The Pistols, when PiL ran out of material they simply played a couple of songs again ('Public Image' and 'Annalisa') –but not before playing two songs from The Pistols' own repertoire, the controversial 'Belsen Was A Gas' and a one-off version of 'Problems'. The success of this show must have put them in fine spirits for the forthcoming London shows.

Prior to the shows both Wobble and Lydon expressed concern regarding the band's likely reception in London. Wobble: "Johnny Rotten is gonna lose, Keith Levene is gonna lose, Jim Walker is gonna lose. And all the kids are gonna watch us get our heads kicked in." Lydon: "I'm going out of my way to even walk out on a stage knowing that three-quarters of the audience won't be there just to listen to us, but to slag us off and survey and suss it out."

The Rainbow Theatre. Christmas Day. The place is packed to the gills with fans awaiting the unveiling. As Wobble, Walker and Levene take to the stage they launch straight into 'Theme', which fills the theatre with a crushing, monstrous, punishing sound. The stage looks fantastic ... all green and black. Finally Lydon saunters on carrying two extremely full carrier bags containing his own supply of lager for the set. But this is more Brunel than Screen On The Green: confrontation not participation. Lydon tries the route of participation by handing the microphone out during 'Theme' for occasional disorientating shouts of 'I wish I could die' from assorted members of the audience. The monumental sound finally dies down. At last the audience can make themselves heard: 'Submission', 'Anarchy In The UK', 'Pretty Vacant'. Lydon gets straight to the point: "We're not gonna play any fucking Sex Pistols songs. If you wanna hear that, fuck off! That's history." 'Lowlife'. Then 'Attack' and the NF skins who have been threatening throughout finally succeed in starting a fight. The band stop and Lydon shakes his head, 'You never learn'.

"The crowd was getting more and more confused and restless between numbers as their relationship with the band became more and more remote from the usual performer-audience axis. Lydon would spend five minutes or more between songs in intense arguments with interjectors." 'Lydon's Return' by Keith Shadwick.

Some jerk at the front gobs right in Lydon's face. Lydon leans down and gobs right back. Unfortunately he hits the guy in front of the jerk; leaning over he flicks the frozen phlegm off the guy's shoulder onto the jerk behind, then apologises to the guy in front.

The Sex Pistols/'78.

Those at the front keep screaming for Johnny to give 'em some cans of lager. He finally obliges, dispensing several cans into the audience. However he gets one back, unopened, full force and right in the face. Blood trickles down where the can hit him. Lydon stands over the stage, "Come on mate. Just you and me. The bouncers won't touch you." There is no response.

"But the real focus of the event was outside the music. It was in the battle between a man and his own public image, this being a microcosm of the central conflict in rock. Here was one of the great figures of his time desperately trying to state clearly his own control of himself." 'Lydon's Return'.

'Public Image' is the encore, though the band never actually leave the stage. Levene, Wobble and Walker are as amazed as anybody by the virulence of the response. But Lydon remains after the encore. As he walks to the side of the stage many members of the audience refuse to leave. Those crowding to the front are now in two camps, on the left PiL supporters, on the right those who came to harangue the man. Lydon is suitably snide, sarcastically putting down those on the right with, "your pink vinyl singles and your *Great Rock 'n' Roll Swindles*", and so the (admittedly futile) lecture continues. But he has already left them behind.

The reviews of the show were remarkably black and white. Mostly black. *Sounds* devoted a whole page to a review of the show, 'The Image Has Cracked' written by someone who opened his review with, "although the album was disappointing 'Low Life' and bits of 'Religion' were good" (clearly a true fan) and spent most of the second half blaming the band for the fact that he couldn't get a taxi after the gig so had to, "walk home in the early morning rain," (actually it wasn't raining). I think the word is 'hatchet-job'. Meanwhile so-called punk fanzine *Ripped And Torn* decided not to mince words with Lydon: "You fucking pathetic little puppet with your totally indulgent wallowing mess of an album ... and your wanky little statements about 'never being a punk'." I think this one was standing stage-right at the end of the concert.

After all this controversy the following night's show passed without any real incident. It is something of a shame that this show became the bootleg album, 'Extra Issue'. Public Image would not play London again for five years, and when PiL finally did appear in 1983 they bore no resemblance to the idealistic band which played The Rainbow that Christmas of 1978. Only Lydon would remain in 1983 – and he would be a changed man.

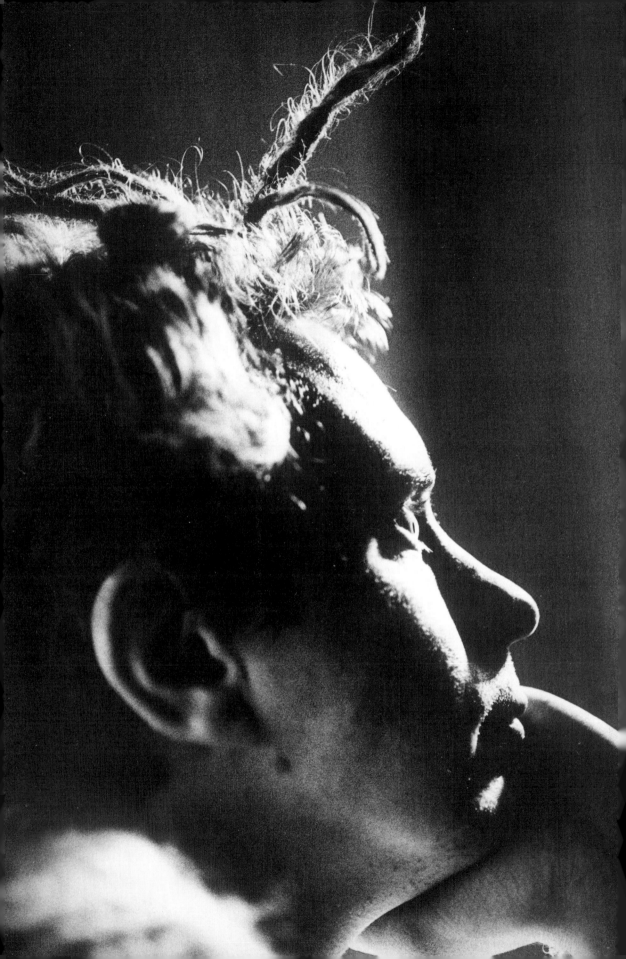

CHAPTER 3

'They expected the band to be an extension of the Pistols and it wasn't'

The first to leave was Jim Walker who, after four gigs at the sticks, called it quits early in the new year. Walker was to be the first of an endless procession of drummers to leave PiL. Though he played far fewer gigs and recorded less albums than Martin Atkins he was the finest drummer to have graced the band, and was never adequately replaced. The official line on his quitting was the tried and tested: "dissatisfaction with musical direction in the group structure." He subsequently helped form The Pack, and was later reunited with Wobble in The Human Condition.

Prior to his departure, Walker recorded one further song with PiL, 'Home Is Where The Heart Is' at the January 1979 sessions. The band were re-recording 'First Issue' for their US label Warner Brothers who were unhappy with the English release. 'Home Is Where The Heart Is' was over-dubbed and partly re-recorded in November 1980 and finally issued on the B-side of the 'Flowers Of Romance' single. It would appear that Walker's contribution remained intact.

Walker's departure presented a fairly major problem. The band had planned "a series of one-off appearances", the first of which, at the Dublin Project Arts Centre on February 16, had already been announced. This problem was compounded by the prospect of legal proceedings brought by Lydon against Malcolm McLaren and Glitterbest coinciding with the scheduled Dublin gig. Inevitably the show was cancelled.

However the band still intended to proceed with a show at Manchester's King's Hall on February 23, which was in aid of the Race Today Friendly Society, and was christened 'Creation For Liberation'. Their first intended replacement for Walker was Vivian Jackson, who had previously appeared on Linton Kwesi Johnson's 'Dread Beat An' Blood' album. It would appear he lasted only a matter of days and made no recordings with the band.

He was succeeded by Dave Humphrey from Hackney who joined only a couple of days prior to the Manchester gig. Indeed at the Manchester show 'Belsen Was A Gas' collapsed due to a lack of rehearsal, much to Lydon's amusement.

Lydon's comment: "Fuckin' egg on face time."

Lydon was simultaneously involved in a seven-day hearing in London regarding the winding up of Glitterbest, proceedings commencing on February 6. The court case received considerable media attention from both the national and music press, and finally concluded on February 14 when the judge ordered a Receiver be appointed to safeguard the assets of Glitterbest.

During these proceedings Lydon was also subject to an uncalled-for police raid on his home at 6.30 am on February 13, apparently the second such raid in a month. Though Lydon was taken to Chelsea Police Station he was released without charges being preferred. Such petty harassment was apparently a regular feature of life for Lydon in Chelsea.

The Manchester show must have proved light relief for the band and despite the drummer's unfamiliarity with the material, the show was a sharp contrast to the London shows the previous December. The audience was very enthusiastic and the band responded with a magnificent second version of 'Annalisa' as an encore. Asked shortly afterwards which PiL gig had been the best, Lydon replied, "Manchester was best, the sound is second to the atmosphere. Up North the shit didn't mean much. They either like it or hate it. They liked PiL. Only in London do we get Sex Pistols requests, ha, ha."

Even the reviews were far more favourable than the Rainbow shows. The overly-pretentious Paul Morley got it exactly right for once when reviewing the show for *NME*: "PiL play it blank and cryptic, offering no easy clues or anything tangible to grab hold of. They satirise, ridicule, delude and elude. It's a joke, a challenge, an indulgence, an assertion, a revenge, an adventure, a disturbance, a fascinating rock 'n' roll sound. You take it seriously or you don't. Whichever way, they're incredibly important." Even *Sounds* reviewer Mick Middles wrote: "I left totally convinced that Public Image are more than a major force in today's music scene."

The band remained surprisingly active. Despite having completed their début album only a couple

Rainbow – December, 1978.

of months previously, PiL were soon back in the studio working on further material. Recording at Jah Studio, presumably with Humphrey at the drums, the band taped a "modern version of Tchaikovsky's *Swan Lake*." In fact Lydon's mother had died recently, and the harrowing song (better known as 'Death Disco') proved an anguished description of Lydon's feelings after losing someone very close to him.

Once again Lydon, Wobble and Levene decided that Dave Humphrey was not exactly what the band had in mind so they sought a fourth drummer in less than six months. Their final selection was Richard Dudanski (formerly of The 101'ers and The Raincoats), a solid time-keeper who was excited by the prospect of working with such a potentially ground-breaking band.

By May Dudanski was ensconced in the studio and the bulk of the recordings for PiL's second album were completed between May and July. Certainly recorded at this time were 'And No Birds

Do Sing', 'Albatross', 'Memories' and 'Chant'. Probably also dating from this period were 'Another' and 'Socialist'. Along with 'Death Disco' these numbers would account for well over half of 'Metal Box'.

As a mildly humorous interlude from such exertions Lydon agreed to be a guest on the BBC's revival of *Juke Box Jury*, hosted by the faintly nauseating Noel Edmunds. Asked by Edmunds what music he listened to, Lydon replied, "My own." Throughout the show he acted like a delinquent modern-day Groucho Marx, and eventually he grew bored with the whole thing and made one of his famous impromptu stage-exits – though apparently the camera missed it. He had to come back and do it again.

More importantly the band played its second gig of the year – in Manchester again, though this time it was a secret gig only announced on the day. It took place on June 18 at Russell's Club (perhaps better known as The Factory), in

Manchester's seedy Moss Side district, and a wealth of new songs were premiered. In their one-hour set the band featured only two songs from the first album, 'Public Image' (which they had to try three times before getting it right) and 'Annalisa'.

The new songs performed were extended versions of 'Chant', 'Death Disco', 'Memories', 'And No Birds Do Sing' (into which Lydon interjected several couplets of 'Arsenal 3 'Nited 2' as a taunt to the – few – United fans there, Arsenal having beaten Manchester United in an historic Cup Final by that score-line the previous month) and 'Albatross'. As with the February show the whole affair was good humoured, and was a successful 'rehearsal' for Richard Dudanski.

Eleven days later the band released their second single, 'Death Disco'. The seven-inch version featured a four-minute edited version of the song, and included 'And No Birds Do Sing' (featuring Dudanski on drums) on the B-side. However the 12-inch version featured an alternate B-side, an instrumental version of 'Fodderstompf' (entitled 'half mix'), and an astonishing unedited 11-minute version of 'Death Disco' on the A-side.

Of this 12-inch version Melody Maker's Chris Bohn wrote at the end of 1979, when 'Death Disco' was voted single of the year: "'Mega Mix' (sic), the song's continuation on the 12-inch, fully justifies the extravagance of the extra vinyl, it being the most awesome and complete musical experience since Can's 'Tago Mago'. Most importantly, though, it's the one dance single of the year to define its own style, without shaping someone else's to suit its own needs."

The single also revealed that the group were veering away from the commercial sound of 'Public Image' towards the organised chaos of 'Theme'. Not surprisingly, despite a further bout of critically favourable reviews and an appearance on Top Of The Pops (where they performed the song live in the studio), 'Death Disco' proved substantially less successful than 'Public Image', barely cracking the Top 20.

The band also appeared on a new Tyne-Tees TV programme at the beginning of July, promo-ting 'Death Disco' by playing a live version of 'Chant' in the studio but after their one-song performance they were again the subject of a cheap publicity stunt. The naïve presenters of 'Check It Out' inserted a film of Mond Cowie of the talentless (and thankfully long-forgotten) Angelic Upstarts bad-mouthing 'Johnny Rotten' – without PiL's prior knowledge – and then asked Lydon for his response. Needless to say the response was blunt and to the point – Lydon told the young and unprofessional presenters that it was, "a cheap-skate comedy interrogation act and it just ain't on," and duly walked off – this time for real.

At this point Wobble challenged the presenters to think of a vaguely intelligent question and then let out a stream of wholly justified (and duly censored) abuse before detaching his mike and storming off. Jeanette Lee later summed up the feelings of the PiL camp when asked by NME for their version of the incident: "You can understand that the whole cheap affair was an attempt to goad John into doing his nut and giving the show a great deal of publicity. It was sickening."

At the beginning of August Levene and Lydon were interviewed, somewhat more civilly, for Radio Merseyside and Levene took the oppor-tunity to comment on the prejudices the band faced at this point: "At first they expected the band to be an extension of The Pistols and it wasn't, it didn't occur to them to pick up on what PiL was. Instead of that they became kinda intimi-dated by it again – just because we were some-thing different. That's what we get all the time just because they're not prepared. It doesn't occur to them to just pick up on what we are doing. They expect us to start gobbing and spewing up."

Clearly PiL felt the pressure of these false expectations and constantly being called on to defend themselves. In a letter to a fan in August 1979 Lydon spelt out PiL's 'message': "Anything soundwise that breaks the pattern won't even be heard by most and PiL are not a typical sound . . . PiL will win. Rock 'n' roll is dead. It all is . . . Music is collective noises, there must be no limits."

Further interviews in July and August repre-sented a belated attempt to promote 'Death

Disco'. Asked why he should use such a conventional medium as interviews, Lydon baldly stated: "Because I don't want to fade into oblivion and never be heard of again . . . All forms of communication are important. People (must) know you exist."

Likewise, arranging a series of one-off concert appearances by the band secured the greatest exposure for the minimum amount of effort. They consented to headline the first night of the Leeds Sci-Fi Festival on September 8 at the Queen's Hall. It would be PiL's last UK show for four years – and the last UK show to feature Dudanski, Wobble or Levene. The gig itself showcased both old and new material.

However Leeds' response to PiL was as apathetic as their response to The Pistols had been when they played the Polytechnic on the famous Anarchy Tour, and if fans in Manchester didn't shout for Sex Pistols songs they certainly did in Leeds. As if this wasn't bad enough one so-called fan decided to throw a full can of lager, not at Lydon this time but at Wobble. As a result Lydon turned his back on the audience and remained that way throughout the rest of the set, a gesture later misrepresented in press reports of the show.

Indeed the fickle music press once again turned on the band. Andy Gill's review in *NME* failed to identify most of the songs despite the fact that only three of the nine songs had yet to be released ('Chant', 'Memories' and 'Another') while the *Sounds* reviewer betrayed his all-too-obvious prejudice with the comment, "One measly rendition of 'Pretty Vacant' would have converted an expensive extravaganza into a rock 'n' roll concert." It would also have undone all of PiL's work to date. In fact the most negative assessment of the gig came from Levene himself: "We did a shit gig, to a shit audience in a shit place. We had a horrible time."

Only the *Record Mirror* reviewer appreciated the quality of the band, as well as both the flaws and virtues of this particular performance: "At times (particularly on the magnificent 'Death Disco' and 'Annalisa') PiL blended together as a superb unit. Yet generally their sound was as anonymous as Lydon's stage presence."

There were two major and immediate results of the Leeds gig – the departure of Richard Dudanski, and a decision by the band to avoid further UK shows, for the time being at least. Dudanski in fact wrote to the *NME* editor, Neil Spencer, to announce his departure and the reasons behind it:
"Dear Mr Spencer,

In the absence of any statement from PiL, I would like to inform you that as from our Leeds gig I have ceased to be a member of that group.

My disagreements and inability to work with certain members of the group in particular, resulted in mutual satisfaction at my exit.

My only observation is that what could potentially be a great band, will probably do just enough to retain its guaranteed success. Perhaps exactly because of this guarantee, the really good ideas behind the band will never be more than just that. I hope not for JR's sake."

Malcolm McLaren.

CHAPTER 4

'We take a silly tune and strip it bare and start again'

Dudanski's departure did not hinder the completion of the second album. Apparently Levene took it upon himself to record some of the drum tracks in order to complete the album. Certainly PiL continued to record new songs for 'Metal Box' throughout September. In fact it was announced in the press at the end of the month that the album would actually consist of three 12-inch singles, "with an aggregate playing time equivalent to that of a normal LP." It would also come in, "a cross between a film can and a biscuit tin", would be appropriately titled 'Metal Box', and would be released on October 12 with a single, 'Memories', issued the week before.

'Memories' and its B-side, 'Another', had already been recorded with Dudanski. Indeed both songs were performed at the Leeds Sci-Fi Festival. The 'Memories' single was in the shops by October 5 (though the official release date was October 10). It came as no surprise when the album was put back to November 16 as, "not all the tracks have been delivered yet."

Meanwhile the search for a permanent drummer continued. Karl Burns of The Fall apparently rehearsed with the band, and was considered for the job. But in the end it was given to a long-standing fan of PiL, the previously unknown Martin Atkins. His audition was the recording of 'Bad Baby', one of, (if not the) last song to be recorded for 'Metal Box'. Thus the band completed the album and found a drummer – one who would play on all the albums and all but one of their gigs over the next five years.

'Memories' is probably the most inaccessible of all the singles issued under the PiL logo. Though undoubtedly a good indication of the direction the band had headed in with 'Metal Box', it was also highly non-commercial. The review in Sounds summed up many people's view of both the song and the band: "'Memories' is an apt enough title as this brings back memories of all their other rubbish." On the other hand Danny Baker in NME made the record 'Single Of The Week' but also observed: "Certainly no quarter for DJs to waffle out dedications on the airwaves; 'Memories' has no place within today's broad-casting set-up." This proved to be the case and the single reached the none-too-dizzy heights of number 60 in the charts.

The fate of 'Memories' was not a precursor to commercial failure for 'Metal Box'. The fact that the album would have only a limited 50,000 pressing in this 3 x 12-inch 45 format ensured it would receive a short, sharp burst of sales – exactly the type of sales that do well in the album charts. Indeed the album entered the charts at number 18 and stayed in the charts for eight weeks, by which time the initial pressing had near-as-dammit run out.

Album sales were undoubtedly helped by the almost universally ecstatic critical response. Though the band always had a very ambivalent relationship with the UK press – and vice versa – for this one instant the critics were united in their praise of PiL's achievement. Angus MacKinnon perhaps summed up the general response when he wrote of 'Metal Box': "All this forward flow in 12 months – it's almost frightening. PiL are miles out and miles ahead. Follow with care."

Such was the effect of the album that NME actually put the band on the cover, with the headline 'Open the box, take the money – The Public Image Album', with simply the album review and no feature inside. Angus MacKinnon's full-page review made the obvious link between PiL and German avant-garde band Can: "PiL produce the most aggressively – and sometimes oppressively – physical sound on record since Can made 'Monster Movie' or 'Tago Mago'." He also realised that the band's approach to a studio was perhaps the key to the quality of the album: "The PiL noise is a three-way street, a most democratic and co-operative animal that uses the studio as it sees fit, as an additional instrument mostly, that assesses where the limits of the recording technology lie and tends to break beyond them."

Even Sounds, previously the most anti-PiL of the three major UK weekly music papers, devoted a page to the album and Dave McCullough not only gave it five stars (Indispensable), but attempted to evaluate the album's likely future

importance: "'Metal Box' is a vital ending to seventies pop culture and a sizeable nod in the direction of a real rock 'n' roll future. The last laugh is with John Lydon and no mistake." Chris Bohn's review in *Melody Maker* was more restrained, though he was still impressed: "'Metal Box' is simply a progression from and a perfection of 'PiL' (ie 'First Issue')."

Though the album came without printed lyrics, the adverts for it did not. Full page press advertising the album simply carried the band name at the top, the album title at the bottom and the lyrics in between, untitled and randomly placed. With the surprising critical response to the album and the lyrics on full view Lydon faced a new problem perhaps not previously considered – repeated questions as to what this or that song meant. He tried to deflect such comments when interviewed by Trevor Dann for BBC Radio One's *Rock On*. When asked how they write songs he replied: "We take a silly tune and strip it bare and start again."

Though 'Metal Box' was still perceived as an album, it was in fact a very deliberate attempt by the band to get away from that particular medium (though in fact an 'album' of records was originally a box of 78 rpm records which together made up the 'album', much as the three 12-inch singles made up 'Metal Box'). Levene stated, "Bear in mind, it's not an album. You don't have to listen to the songs in any order. You can play what you want, disregard what you don't. Albums have a very strict format, the eight tracks, difficult to find, I hate all that – the quality is usually appallingly low, almost unlistenable. We can't get our sound on a normal record, you can't get the depths and heights."

However if the band wanted to find new ground-breaking ways of reaching the public they still found themselves constrained to promotional interviews such as the aforementioned Radio One's *Rock On*. Levene and Lydon were again required to explain the co-operative nature of the band. Levene: "I say it's John, me and Wobble and we have had various drummers and they've always been told what to do and play. It's just one of those equal things."

1981, Left to right: Johnny Rotten, Jeanette Lee, Keith Levene

In fact the insert with 'Metal Box' credited two other members to 'the company', both long-standing friends and members of the PiL 'family': Dave Crowe and Jeanette Lee. By the time Vivien Goldman interviewed the band for *Melody Maker* in December, Levene was referring to the group as "a unit of five, three public" with "the band bit of PiL as just me (Levene), John and Wobble."

Goldman trying to figure out what Jeanette Lee's role was, observed: "It's Jeanette who does the bulk of liaising with the outside world, as far as I can make out, though everyone in PiL refuses to say exactly what they do . . . Jeanette will (also) be making a film record, a kind of diary, of PiL." Their interest in video techniques was to become a common theme in interviews over the next 18 months. Levene: "We're into vision – video – we've got this Super-8 camera . . . we want to use electronics as special effects, using electronics to condense the quality of the Super-8."

This branching out hinted at by Levene's comment, (and the means by which PiL might achieve it) would become the central dilemma for the band in the coming months. Goldman summed up the essential problem when she concluded her December 1979 article with the observation: "PiL still haven't reached what to me seems the ideal stage: sending a constant stream of communiqués, records or otherwise, that would remove them from the pitfalls of the 'PiL album – an event – articles in the music press soon come' syndrome."

Of course part of the problem was financial. The band had to promote their albums as this was their main source of income. Likewise the occasional gig, on a worthwhile scale, was a highly profitable and not particularly time-consuming exercise. For the Leeds Sci-Fi Festival they reputedly earned £3,000.

It was the exigencies of finance (and the lax way the band handled such matters) which often dictated the band's preferred course of action. They still needed to promote their one definite source of worthwhile income. This resulted in two highly impressive appearances for the BBC in the winter of 1979/80.

In November PiL recorded three songs for a session on John Peel's prestigious late-night show on Radio One. 'Careering' in particular gave the band ample opportunity to improvise new sounds, and to further Levene's increasing pre-occupation with synthesizers. Along with (the much more commercial) 'Poptones', it was also performed on BBC-2's long-running *Old Grey Whistle Test*, now thankfully wrestled from the control of the somnambulant Bob Harris. Martin Atkins confirmed his position as 'new PiL drummer' – the most insecure job in music – by providing the necessary backbone on these two appearances.

However it was in Paris in January that Atkins made his real live début. The band had decided to return to the city which received them so well in 1978, to play two gigs at Parisian night-spot The Palace. It would be the band's first gigs in four months, and both shows were recorded.

Their first concert on January 17 was fine – certainly the better of the two. It was also reviewed by *NME*, and most of the 'Paris Au Printemps' album was recorded on this occasion. According to *NME*'s reviewer Frazer Clarke, "This was an alienating performance, but if it were John Lydon's aim to be a popular success he'd be singing re-treads of 'Pretty Vacant' (sic) . . . We should be grateful."

It was a lengthy set by PiL standards, with 12 songs ('Another' not 'Graveyard' – from 'Metal Box' plus 'Annalisa', 'Public Image', 'Attack' and 'Low Life' from 'First Issue'), clocking in at a full hour. The show also featured live premières of 'Careering', 'Poptones' and 'Bad Baby'. However the audience do not seem to have responded at all enthusiastically and Frazer Clarke confessed he'd, "never before seen a band give an encore after having been jeered off." Indeed Lydon later said the only doctoring of the tapes of these shows used on the live album, 'Paris Au Prin-temps', was "some reverb to drown out the crowd booing."

If the band were unaffected by the crowd on the first night, their brief-to-the-point-of-terse set the following night suggests a certain degree of

mutual hostility. In fact the set lasted a mere seven songs, concluding with 'Theme' (which sadly missed the majestic drumming of Walker).

A month later 'Metal Box' was reissued as 'Second Edition', this time as a double album in a conventional sleeve. This was the format released in the US, where it received a favourable review by Greil Marcus for *Rolling Stone*, the solitary major US bi-weekly music magazine.

Having virtually locked themselves in the recording studio over the previous 18 months, PiL now came up for air. The critical, and to some extent commercial, success of 'Metal Box' allowed them necessary breathing space. The debacle at Leeds in September had precluded any possibility of further UK gigs – at least for the time being – so despite the spectre of The Sex Pistols' final tour, Lydon and Co decided the time had come to take the PiL message to the colonies. In March they set about arranging a US 'visit' (the band refused to call it a tour, though it was as near to a tour as PiL ever came).

For both band and country it would prove a bitter pill to swallow.

CHAPTER 5

'This is one band no-one dictates to – ever.
No routines'

"We're just not over-eager to do live gigs; you only get a lot of thickos who just want to hear rock 'n' roll, even though I know there are some good people out there who want to hear good music, interesting music with subtleties and variations in it."

Jah Wobble – February 1980.

In the early months of 1980, Wobble put together both his first solo album, 'The Legend Lives On' and another mini-album, 'Blueberry Hill', a matter of weeks later. 'The Legend Lives On' in particular was an audacious collection of exercises in sound, with titles like 'Pineapple', the inimitable 'Dan McArthur' and 'Not Another' (which of course sounded suspiciously like PiL's 'Another'). "I (just) wanted to put a sunshine record together, but not be insulting . . . I've got a happy side as well. I hope people tape it off Peel and listen to it by the sunny river," said Wobble.

At this stage Wobble was determined to make clear that his solo projects did not suggest any lessening in his commitment to PiL: "It's partly a political thing in one sense: making your stand.

It's like with PiL we have our own organisation so to speak. PiL is five people really, six now with Martin. There's a girl called Jeanette and Dave Crowe, both of whom are involved, coming up with ideas. PiL is more than just a band; it's an all-embracing attitude."

The solo albums only came about because of Lydon and Levene's absence in the United States in March setting up the PiL's springtime 'visit'. It was also restlessness that produced 'Betrayal': "In PiL strange things happen, you can be sitting about for four months just soaking up influences . . . no one really made a decision to go to America as such."

Lydon and Levene flew to San Francisco at the beginning of March. It was partly a promotional visit coinciding with the US release of 'Second Edition'; partly to arrange a subsequent PiL blitz on the USA, and presumably to test the water. Aside from several interviews the duo appeared on one obscure late-night radio show, *Hepcats From Hell* and conducted a (predictably farcical) press conference at a San Franciscan disco/new wave club called The City.

The press conference was the usual US circus, though it served as a useful indication of how PiL and the US press would (not) get on when the whole band returned a month later. Asked about a tour, Lydon replied: "We'll be doing occasional gigs according to our whims and fancies. This is one band no one dictates to – ever. No routines."

Inevitably most of the questions centred on The Sex Pistols. Q: What is the connection between PiL and The Pistols? A: "There is no connection. The Pistols finished rock 'n' roll. That was the last rock 'n' roll band. It is all over. It's (in) the past." Q: Why if the band was so contemptuous of the media did they consent to the press conference? A: "We need to promote our records. There is no point in hiding in closets and being arty. It is essential that everybody is aware that this band exists, because there is no competition. And I'd like that to be made very clear."

Three one-to-two interviews were conducted in the Continental Hyatt Hotel in LA – Lydon and Levene having flown there from San Francisco – and were somewhat more satisfactory. The most important was with Mikal Gilmore for *Rolling Stone*. Gilmore started by asking Lydon and Levene about their impressions of an American press conference, particularly the endless questions about Lydon's previous band: "All I can say is that Public Image is everything The Sex Pistols were meant to be – a valid threat to rock 'n' roll. In the end The Pistols weren't any more threatening than retreaded Chuck Berry."

Though their first album hadn't been issued in the States – despite the band having actually re-recorded the album at Warner Brothers' request – Levene and Lydon were still clearly concerned that the critical volte-face of the English music press over 'Metal Box' should not be repeated in the States. Lydon: "Now all the critics love us. I don't trust all these people who praise us now. They're the same ones who waited until The Pistols were over before they accepted them."

Gilmore's article in *Rolling Stone* ended with Lydon's own premonition of the futility of what the band was trying to achieve: "I think our cause will be lost, but that won't be so bad, will it? Until then we can do nothing but benefit your dreary little lives."

Certainly the US press seem to have found it relatively difficult to grasp that PiL were not a rock 'n' roll band. In fact Levene denied that PiL were even musicians: "We're not musicians … Our music's got basic structure but it ain't music 'cos I don't use chords on a guitar. Wobble does sing notes on the bass. They amount to sound. I do sound on a synthesizer. We use rhythm tracks for the drums. It's just different, it just isn't music …"

Lydon was prepared to add a further glossary on Levene's non-musical stance: "We don't make music – it's noise, sound. We avoid the term 'music' because of all those assholes who like to call themselves musicians or artists. It's just so phony. We don't give a shit about inner attitude, just as long as it sounds good. We're not some intellectual bunch of freaks. I think we're a very, very valid act. For once in a lifetime a band actually has its own way, its own terms – that would really make extreme music. We just want to make sure you have a choice. I mean, we can only be hated on a large scale."

To prove the validity of this stance, Lydon, Levene, Wobble and Atkins arrived in the States in the middle of April. Though not booked to play night after night, they arranged at least nine dates spread over the second half of April and the first half of May, designed for maximum exposure in major US cities: Atlanta, Chicago, Boston, New York, Philadelphia, Detroit, Los Angeles, Oakland and San Francisco – an unprecedented bout of gigging for PiL. It was nevertheless a considerable change from what their American label, Warner Bros, had in mind. According to Lydon, "It read something like 60 days non-stop gigging in very very small clubs and it just about covered every single possible part of America."

Though the US visit proved ultimately disastrous for the band's long-term future, the shows themselves were among the most innovative and exciting ever seen in the US. In many ways it is a shame that the official live album issued by PiL at the end of 1980 was derived from the January Paris shows rather than a genuine springtime show from the USA. In fact the 'Paris Au Printemps' album was primarily a response to the much more satisfactory double bootleg album, 'Profile' which came from the May 1980 Los Angeles show, and which *Melody Maker* reviewed enthusiastically.

For once critical response to the shows seems to have been favourable. Particularly encouraging (and important) was Kristine McKenna's review of the Los Angeles show in *Rolling Stone*: "What a show it was. The music was immense and primitive, the crowd was horrifying, and Lydon was staggeringly in control every second."

PiL fans at home were also treated to an enthusiastic review of what exactly they were missing, with a report on the New York show in *NME*: "The show does defeat the expectations of a rock band performance in many ways: their approach to pacing is neither the classic strong start, slow down, big build-up-at-the-end scheme, nor the punk pull out all the stops approach. Instead there are long lulls when the music almost becomes a monotonous flow; then comes the peaks, redeeming everything – not through virtuosity but through daring."

Undoubtedly one of the most daring aspect of the shows was the way Lydon attempted total audience participation. There was a certain incredulity in the tone of *NME*'s reviewer when he reported, "After a while, Lydon starts bringing kids up on-stage to be guest vocalists. When a crowd of nine or 10 punky-looking kids has massed, he hands a music stand and lyric sheet to one of them and joins the kids in the crowd on-stage, just bopping around, grinning broadly. Tonight, his plan to share the stage with his audience causes the set to finally self-destruct – a conclusion which to PiL is probably more than acceptable."

Likewise the *Rolling Stone* reviewer was moved to comment on a similar occurrence at the LA show. "When Lydon picked an adolescent boy out of the audience, brought him on-stage and did a duet with him on 'Bad Baby' and 'Public Image'."

Claude Bessy's review of the same show (for *Slash* magazine) commented much more fully on this inversion of the star/audience role:

"The kid is lifted to the stage and John starts whispering in his ear (no doubt professional tips on stage presence) while handing him a notebook of lyrics. The song is 'Bad Baby' and soon the 'don't you listen' chorus is being sung by the new vocalist over and over again, first with John and then alone. The hecklers, the fans, the spitters – everyone is standing, at a loss for an appropriate response. John sits grinning by the drum set, puffing on a cigarette, while the rest of PiL endlessly repeat the riff.

"The spitting has stopped, this substitution of targets being after all very upsetting and most unlike the way things had to be. And to the dismay of a mob that can't wait for the various roles of star and audience to be reinstated, so they can go on being idol and fan, things don't go back to normal . . . Lydon skanks, laughing, enjoying this holiday, spots a clinging figure to one side and helps a second junior punk to the stage. Number two understands the new game and immediately struts about giving the finger to his mates, spitting on top of their heads and arrogantly skanking and weaving in the Huntingdon Beach Downhill Racer fashion. Two more minutes and a third edition who specialises in the worm style of dancing, the three extras taking turns banging on Keith's synthesizer.

"Lydon announced, "That's it, we've had enough", and bids farewell to Los Angeles. One by one they let go of the riff, Wobble clowns around with the beach representative and reality settles around everyone."

Of course Lydon had given the microphone to members of the audience at previous PiL shows, but he had never undermined the traditional star-fan roles as successfully or as extensively as in the States. Indeed the most unmusical, discordant moment of these US shows was when at the gigs in late April the band played that sinuous beat to 'Fodderstompf' and Lydon handed the mike from fan to fan for a series of 'We only wanted to be loved'. This positively scary series of vocals then

LA Civic Auditorium May 5, 1980 – John Lydon gets a fan to sing for him.

segued into Lydon's own pained rendition of the haunting 'Death Disco'.

Whereas previous shows in England had been, at least in Leeds and London, open confrontations between band and audience, these shows saw a band constantly turning the audience's preconceptions upside down. Just as the audience became comfortable with the disorienting sounds, the band would play the instantly accessible 'Public Image', 'Lowlife' or 'Attack', before returning to more cryptic tunes such as 'Memories'. Meanwhile Lydon would continue his repeated taunts at the punks who had come to spit and gawp at Johnny Rotten – challenging them all the while.

PiL's first show – at The Orpheum in Boston – was the longest gig they ever played. As with the Paris show they played through the four-month rust from lack of gigs, performing some 17 songs and excluding only 'Religion' from their full set. Indeed the band played all the remaining songs from 'First Issue' plus seven songs from 'Second Edition'. They also featured 'Home Is Where The Heart Is', a song new to the PiL live set, though it had been originally recorded with Jim Walker.

The Boston show had been prefaced by two radio interviews/phone-ins on the WBCN-FM and WERS-FM radio stations. Both affairs were fairly well-humoured though the WBCN appearance generally revolved around the band personally abusing anyone foolish enough to phone in. According to an announcement on the WBCN show (conducted on April 16) the band were also due to appear on a local TV station (Channel Five) that night. The stint in Boston seemed to set the routine for the band's remaining shows, with a series of promotional media appearances and interviews announcing that 'PiL were in town'.

CHAPTER 6

'We're not necessarily out there to give people a good time'

The cracks in the 'public image' were fairly quick in coming. At the end of the first US show, Wobble and Atkins played an instrumental continuation of 'Bad Baby' which did not appear to be rehearsed. According to *Subway News*, "After Levene eventually stamped off stage in prima donna fury over the Orpheum speakers and Lydon followed him to thrash things out collective style, Wobble allowed himself to have some ordinary fun with the crowd, mugging like a comic-book gangster and doing a little strutting, smiling and waving."

All along Lydon's attitude to gigging seemed fairly clear-cut. It should be "free form. We decide what songs we do as we do them, as we're inspired. I couldn't bear a fuckin' format." However it would appear that Wobble and Atkins were not entirely happy with the lack of professionalism occasionally displayed on stage by Lydon and Levene.

During PiL's sojourn in Los Angeles in May, Sylvie Simmons asked Lydon whether he shouldn't be doing something for the audience: "In other words dictate? No. I merely offer my point of view and Wobble offers his and you either appreciate it or hate it, simple, but don't slavishly idolise it. I'm not saying I'm totally right." Here was the first hint that Lydon and Wobble might not always agree on PiL-related matters.

Another PiL interview conducted with Levene in Los Angeles, by Bill Bartell, includes a comment about the recording of a new album – but one which would only feature Levene and Lydon: "Well I want to do an album here, release an album out there (waves hand towards LA). It won't be a Public Image album, well it will be, but it will be just me and John on it."

Levene also sought to emphasise the importance of completely spontaneous performances when PiL were on stage: "PiL is a company, a group of people like Jeanette who is in the band, we're individuals and we've got creative output, and this is what we're doing at the moment. We're just trying to use all the companies positively. And when we *do* do gigs, we're not necessarily out there to give people a good time. I just do whatever happens, at the time. It has to be spontaneous."

This view was clearly not in accordance with Wobble's. In 1982 Wobble commented on this American visit in these terms: "The gigs in America, playing for 20 minutes and getting into this corny audience conflict situation – it wasn't leading anywhere. A performer has got a responsibility, especially in ritual music like PiL played. It's give and take."

During their visit to Los Angeles, the band also made its first nationwide US TV broadcast, appearing on Dick Clark's *American Bandstand*. This performance – though mimed – was surprisingly effective, with Lydon "dressed in an oversized white suit plus Hawaiian shirt . . . (as) he bullied *Bandstand*'s usually seated audience of star struck disco kids into joining him on the studio floor."

"He scurries up the other side and drags down another lump of spandex, then another, till finally all the hired dancers and would-be stars are dancing and dayglo-ing everywhere like some horrible infestation, completely blocking the band who mime on, straight-faced, while John is pied-pipering behind the balconies and falling over in delight." 'PiL In Hollywood' (*Sounds* May 1980).

After their stint in LA, PiL headed on to San Francisco for their final two shows at the Oakland Coliseum and San Francisco's Market Centre. The day of the last US gig the band were again participating in a phone-in, on San Rafael's KTIM radio station. But by now the image had clearly cracked.

To the acute embarrassment of Lydon, drummer Martin Atkins took the opportunity of KTIM's live radio programme to launch an attack upon 'the PiL attitude'. Initially he was asked about the solo single that he had recently recorded as Brian Brain, "I just wanted to do something that was slightly professional." The inevitable question followed: "Are you implying that the work you do with PiL is not professional?"

"Yes. I would call it unprofessional. I would call it the emperor's new clothes."

(Lydon: "Go on, Martin. Keep waffling.")

"We are the emperor's new clothes but no one is

saying that we are. We are it.''

"Is Johnny the emperor?''

"No, nobody is the emperor. We are it. I'm just waiting for some fucking asshole to say that we are not wearing any clothes. I just wish somebody would have the fucking guts to do it.''

"What makes it unprofessional?''

"The attitude behind it. The promotion. Lack of management.''

"You manage yourselves?''

"We don't manage ourselves. We mismanage ourselves.''

(Lydon: "Are you still waffling?'')

"Before a gig we unsynchronise our watches, which is the whole crux of it. We cock-up everything there is to cock-up. We constantly underachieve.''

(Lydon (in childish voice): "Can you put a record on, now, now, now?'').

Later on in the show Lydon refers to Atkins as "the embarrassment of our little group'' and Atkins retorts, "Yeah, 'cos I'm professional.'' One other exchange maybe suggested that Lydon and Wobble were also not getting on too well:

DJ: "How was the album constructed? Was it put together in the studio?''

JW: "Yeah. Over a period of about 15 months.''

JL: "Try seven months.''

JW: "It was more than seven months,'' (repeated several times).

JL: "It wasn't. 'Cos of the first album, remember? We had to re-record the first (album) for Warners.''

JW: "I did rhythm tracks for that (second album) at the same time.''

Though the final US show passed without incident it was a very different PiL that returned to Albion. Not surprisingly Atkins was sacked from the band on their return. According to Atkins' own statement, "Jah Wobble might be leaving the group as well.'' However a Virgin statement insisted Wobble was still very much part of the organisation, and that Atkins was "not working with the band any more, as they don't need a drummer because they're not gigging any more." The Virgin statement further insisted that the PiL organisation, "is very much alive. They are working on other visual and aural projects, the fruits of which will be seen and heard shortly."

Whatever the official Virgin line was, PiL were clearly self-destructing. The statement that the band would be playing no more gigs cannot have met with Wobble's approval. In fact Levene and Lydon flew out to the States at the end of June (minus Wobble) for further discussions on the possibility of a film soundtrack, first mooted by Levene during the American visit in May (and something Wobble was not likely to be involved in), and to appear on another networked US TV show, Tom Synder's *Tomorrow Show* on NBC.

The comments made by Levene and Lydon on this show suggested that the possibility of PiL playing any future gigs was remote. Lydon told Snyder he considered gigs nowadays as, "a bunch of gits on a stage with all these idiots standing in the pits worshipping them, thinking they're heroes. There should be no difference between who's on stage and who's in the audience. And we've tried very hard to break down those barriers but it's not working . . . so we have to think again and in the meantime we'll put our attention somewhere else."

A further comment by Levene made it clear that it was the band's recent US visit which prompted this rethink. "We ended up doing an American tour which definitely prompted us to stop the band side of things and concentrate on the company side of things."

The *Tomorrow* interview rapidly became an extremely bad-tempered affair, with Snyder totally uncomprehending, a thoroughly unsuitable (if typical) American chat-show host. As such Lydon was quick to put Snyder down even when he occasionally asked a perfectly sensible question, while Levene just sat there throughout looking exceedingly stoned, or jet-lagged, or both. When The Pistols were finally mentioned Lydon stage-whispered, "I wondered when you'd get to that."

During the commercial break (taken halfway through the interview) Synder apparently ex-

ploded: "What the fuck are you doing? You're making a fucking fool of yourself." Lydon later contended that he'd been set up and was heard to describe Snyder as a "fuckin' cunt" and "a wanker".

However justified Lydon and Levene may have been in their belief that Snyder was the most uncomprehending interviewer they had yet faced, Lydon's petulant behaviour on national TV was not well-received by American press and public alike. *Rolling Stone* reported that, "Snyder, for once, was right on the mark," when calling Lydon a "fucking fool" and "no one could figure out why," the duo had agreed to appear on the show. Clearly this was not a particularly successful exercise in the art of communication from a so-called communication company.

The day prior to flying to New York, Levene organised another PiL communiqué – an interview with *NME* regarding the current situation within the band, possibly intended as an attempt to abate mounting speculation over their future. Unfortunately the front-cover of the edition featuring the interview carried the headline: 'The PiL Corp to cease trading?' In the interview Levene

Tom Snyder

again referred to his desire to secure the film soundtrack offered back in May, by director Michael *Woodstock* Wadleigh, for his forthcoming film the subject-matter of which was to be the "similarities between wolves and Red Indians – their outsider sensibilities, pack hunting and instinctive behaviour."

"I met loads of guys in America who spoke about PiL, but he (Wadleigh) was the only one who knew what he was talking about," said Levene. "He's the only one who could pick up on those 32 levels ('of different things you can get off in PiL music') I was talking of earlier; he could pinpoint and talk about them on certain tracks."

Some kind of deal had apparently already been reached: "He offered us a third of the soundtrack and I hope that we impress him enough (so) that we can do all of it. He wants us in our music to possibly find sounds for what a wolf sees and hears and smells when it sees a human and so on. We might just end up doing vocal sounds through John and treating them."

When talking about the band Levene was happy to state that . . . "What John wants to do and what I want to do are similar, so talking about me is like talking about me and John. I just wanted to put the points over, because John won't talk at length." However the only mention of Wobble was an attack on his solo album, using the (later oft-quoted) charge that Wobble had used PiL backing tracks on his solo album, though only 'Not Another' features a clearly discernible PiL sound:

"We can all do solo work, yeah, but it comes under PiL, not Jah Wobble. We always knew that Wobble was making the record, but we didn't know anything about it, so I don't see that it connects with PiL at all – whereas I see any of the stuff I do as always connecting with PiL. The thing that Wobble did was a mercenary act. I didn't like him using backing tracks from PiL that I didn't want people to hear."

In view of this, it came as no surprise when Wobble announced later in July that he had left the band, though initially the split was reported to be amicable. Clearly this was untrue as Wobble's rift with Lydon never healed, and their years of friendship came to an unpleasant end. Looking back on his departure a couple of years later Wobble had this to say: "Public Image was always Rotten's vehicle. I figured that out. It took about nine months for me to decide to leave and it was finally because I couldn't stand the pretentiousness of it all . . . it was supposed to be an umbrella organisation, which it never became. The video, our own label, none of that ever happened. I started to feel embarrassed."

Wobble himself recruited old PiL drummer Jim Walker from The Pack to help form a new band called The Human Condition. His work since leaving PiL has remained thought-provoking and always rhythmic. And, though drummers were probably replaceable, Wobble was not. Levene and Lydon wisely chose not to replace him. However they had not as yet resolved how the band could maintain any kind of public profile without a rhythm section.

While Lydon and Levene decided which direction PiL should go in, their only recourse in order to maintain a public profile – and to fund future ventures when new product was not forthcoming – was the tried and tested live album. With no Christmas release on the horizon, PiL decided on this ironic gesture to previous incarnations – a potted history of PiL as an occasional live band. Lydon though was quick to point out that the release of 'Paris Au Printemps' – on the first anniversary of the release of 'Metal Box' – was simply an anti-bootlegging exercise: "It's a hell of a lot cheaper than the bootleg and much better quality – that's it." Of course PiL received royalties, which they didn't with bootlegs.

In fact Lydon's comments did make some kind of sense as out of the band's total of 18 gigs so far some four bootleg albums (including one double) had been pressed up (from Paris, London, Leeds and LA respectively), an indication of the band's extraordinary cult status. Unfortunately, impressive as the live album is, it compares unfavourably with the 'Profile' double album drawn from the far more audacious American shows.

Inevitably the reviews of the live album all commented on the contradiction involved in PiL

Jeanette Lee and friend, John Lydon and Ariup's mum.

even issuing something as mundane as a live album. Equally inevitably the review in *Sounds* was the most damning, Dave McCullough's thrupenny-worth consisting of statements like, "An album of blank noise would have said more about PiL, been more redeeming than this lifeless lump of rehashed vinyl."

At the other extreme Lynden Barber in *Melody Maker* wrote that, "the music here is guaranteed to affect you like no other music you've ever come across. It's dangerous nightmare music that'll make you worry, lifting the stone of normality to find the dirt lurking beneath." Lydon's own sardonic comment on reading this review was, "Well that's enough to turn off anyone. I mean would you buy a record that promised to sound like that." Meanwhile Vivien Goldman commented on, "Wobble's steady bass, teetering on the brink of nimble jazz runs" and concluded, "The biggest question raised by the 'Paris Au Printemps' time capsule is – what will PiL be minus Wobble?" Aye, what indeed!

CHAPTER 7

'Who would want to listen to me whining in self pity'

While Lydon and Levene searched for a future direction for the PiL corporation, Lydon decided to join his brother's band 4" Be 2" for a weekend in Dublin at the beginning of October 1980. Though it was expected that the odd pint would be consumed Lydon couldn't have envisaged that he would be charged with assaulting a pub owner and his assistant, "both seven feet tall and six feet wide", Eamonn Brady and Eamonn Leddy respectively. Lydon later stated that he was considering relocating PiL enterprises to Ireland. The incident was a major disincentive.

Lydon wandered into the Horse And Tram pub on October 3 with an anonymous fan who offered to buy him a drink. After being refused service, Lydon allegedly became abusive and physically assaulted the pub's owner and assistant. Lydon's own account of the incident was somewhat different:

"This man asked me for an autograph out in the street and offered me a pint of beer. Well, we went up to the bar and asked for two pints of lager and were told 'no'. When we were told to get out I asked him why. Was I black or something? He just told me to get out. Then, when I was walking out I got smashed in the back of the head . . . I have never been in any sort of affray like that. I've been beaten up by National Front supporters but I've never been in anything like that."

Lydon was forced to spend the whole weekend in Dublin's notorious Mountjoy Prison after a District Court judge, Justice McCarthy, turned down three pleas for bail on Saturday. On the Monday afternoon he was sentenced to three months in jail at which point a Virgin representative put up the necessary bail pending an appeal against the decision, to be heard in December.

The affair certainly contributed to Lydon's increasing sense of disillusionment with life in the British Isles. Despite insisting he would not write about his weekend in jail – "That would be too corny. How could I write about me like that. Who would want to listen to me whining in self-pity?" – 'Francis Massacre' on the 'Flowers Of Romance' album, though ostensibly about the life sentence of Francis Moran, retained the refrain, 'Mountjoy is fun/ Go down for life.'

At the beginning of November Lydon and Levene, with Martin Atkins (re-hired on a day-to-day basis), headed for Virgin's Manor Studios in Oxford to start work on the follow-up to the monumental 'Metal Box'. Though supposedly there to record some demos with producer Mick Glossop, work commenced – albeit tortuously – on the album proper. According to Levene:

"It was just me, John and Jeanette in the studio, and Martin Atkins, who went on tour with us. We were booked into The Manor for 10 days and it was like we knew we were doing a new album, and we couldn't do anything for days – we couldn't do anything. It was like this horrible mental block. After wasting seven days of being waited on hand and foot, just being real lazy cunts . . . we were really trying but nothing was happening. It was something to do with The Manor as well. We did get one track down – 'Hymie's Hymn' – that was the first definite solid thing we got laid down."

Levene spent two days at The Manor, "painstakingly trying to redo" 'Home Is Where The Heart Is' using a loop of four notes on the bass to replace Wobble's original contribution. The song ended up as the B-side of the 'Flowers Of Romance' single. Three songs featuring Atkins, 'Four Enclosed Walls', 'Under The House' and 'Banging The Door', presumably also date from The Manor sessions.

Sessions continued at Townhouse Studios on Goldhawk Road in West London, primarily with the intention of mixing the album down, though Lydon and Levene continued to record further material. Chris Salewicz, interviewing Lydon and Levene, described the scene that greeted him:

"John is hunched over a 32-track mixing desk that dwarfs his slight, unexpectedly studious figure. He is mixing PiL tracks recorded the previous day for a new studio album. Between takes, from time to time, he peers up at the television that is set in the wall above his head."

It was really at the Townhouse that the duo devised the sound they wanted – a new sound for PiL. At various stages of the project they seemed uncertain of the final sound the album would

Top of the pops, April 1981.

have, though as Levene later commented, "We knew we were gonna concentrate on the drum sound."

After three weeks rigorous work Levene realised the sound was fine, and that further overdubs were unnecessary: "There were two weeks when we were doing this album at the Townhouse. We had this fucking great drum sound and we had all these tracks. I was racking my brains – what can I put on this? What can I put on that? And I kept listening back to them. On the last day, we knew we weren't gonna have any more time for it so we were finishing it off, it was then I realised – fuck it, that's it! There's no room for anything. And that was a track that might only have had the drums, John's voice, and that's all."

Though Levene was uncertain what sound he did want, he was certain what sound he did not want – that of 'Metal Box': "If you restrict yourself to labels like rock 'n' roll you're never going to get anywhere with PiL . . . That's my dilemma in the studio right now. Right this minute. The last album, 'Metal Box', if you want to call it rock 'n' roll, it's the furthest you can go in rock 'n' roll . . . Now there's got to be a complete change. At the moment I'm designing a drum synthesizer that I'd like to put out on the market."

Though the album was completed by the end of November, it would not be released for some five months. Looking back on 'Flowers Of Romance' in 1982, Lydon felt that it was recorded too quickly and at a bad time personally for him: "I came straight out of jail in Dublin and came to London and recorded instantly . . . (As for 'Go Back') that's the way I was feeling at the time, and it shows badly. It's horrible to listen back to that kind of paranoia."

Lydon returned to Dublin for his appeal against the sentence dished out to him in October. Perhaps fearing the worst, he was mightily surprised when after only a five-minute hearing in the Circuit Court, Judge Frank Martin granted the appeal against the sentence, acquitting Lydon of the charge against him. Judge Martin stated he was, "Satisfied of the petty nature of the incident and of the fact that neither of the publicans had been injured in the alleged fracas."

In December a few select journalists heard some of the new PiL studio album, scheduled for January or February release. Ian Penman previewed the album in *NME* with the headline 'PiL's Ukulele Album' and obtained one intriguing quote from Lydon regarding the new sound: "Minimalism. Everything just plays on dynamics. No tune is played, there is no melody going through any song. We just piled a load of instruments in the corner of the studio and thought what can we do with this?"

49

Despite certain worrying implications that seem with hindsight implicit in Lydon's comments, Penman quickly defended the material he had heard – four songs – observing that, "the resulting noises certainly do not lack melody or discipline."

Penman was positively reserved compared to the hyperbole gushing from Vivien Goldman's normally restrained pen as she referred to the new studio album at the end of her review of 'Paris Au Printemps':

"Instead of Levene stepping into the bassie slot, as I'd expected, PiL have done it again, broken another sound barrier. While half the world wants to sound like Chic, and the other half like Sly and Robbie – or like PiL, come to that – the Company's created a new kind of rhythm, a definite dance-able rhythm not based on bass and drums . . . The meaning behind the moaning gets clearer all the time."

The band played the title-track, 'Flowers Of Romance', on their third interview for Radio One's *Rock On* at the end of November – ostensibly arranged to promote the 'Paris Au Printemps' album. It would be over four months before fans would hear the rest of the album.

Though Virgin had been very keen to get PiL's first two albums out, this was clearly not the case with 'Flowers Of Romance'. The live album had dropped out of the charts after just two weeks, peaking at number 61, so there was no question of the two albums competing for sales. PiL's relationship with Virgin had always been an at-arms-length arrangement, the label seemingly only tolerating PiL because it was John Lydon's band. Now relations discernibly deteriorated.

Part of the problem was financial. All the band's ideas and schemes would come to naught without the necessary finance, and clearly the only money Virgin was prepared to advance was on the basis of records produced – preferably ones they could sell. Which of course was also a problem. PiL had never been a commercial band, even if their avant-garde approach had engendered support among a certain critical coterie. However Virgin was, for once, fully justified in considering much of the material on 'Flowers Of Romance' even less accessible than previous excursions.

Even Lydon admitted as much when he told *Record Mirror*: "I'd have to say that if 'Flowers' had made the top I'd seriously have to question: 'Why?' That sort of mass acceptance can be an indication of 'Oh my God! – the world's caught up with us, or we've gone three steps back'."

Virgin's decision to delay the release of the album made no sense at all. Apparently they considered the album so uncommercial that they felt they, "should first re-release the group's 'Public Image' début single to stimulate interest in it." When Virgin finally agreed to the album's release, they were only initially interested in a small pressing, much to Levene's considerable chagrin:

"We've got to get this record out and get it promoted but like Virgin are only pressing up 20,000 records (apparently they actually pressed 30,000). They say they'll press up more when it's sold but if a record is not in when someone wants it, four out of seven won't go back."

Ironically, after Virgin's reservations, the album proved to be PiL's highest album chart entry to date. Of course this was primarily due to the hit single released two weeks prior to the album. However it was not 'Public Image', but the title track of the album which provided PiL with their third Top 30 single.

In fact 'Flowers Of Romance' reached 24 in the singles charts – boosted by a particularly surreal appearance on *Top Of The Pops*. Lydon was dressed like a defrocked vicar, Jeanette Lee sawed away at double bass, and Levene resembled a half-crazed medic beating away at the drums. Boosted by the success of the single the album charted at 11, seven places higher than 'Metal Box', though it only remained in the charts for five weeks. Clearly the core of PiL fans remained essentially unchanged in size and persuasion.

Reviews of the album were curiously mixed. Every extreme was catered for, from Lynden Barber (again) in *Melody Maker* who stated: "Whatever your attitude towards PiL . . . it's an album that demands to be heard by everybody who claims to be concerned about contemporary music. If there's a more innovative record released during the next 12 months I'll be astonished," to Jeff Nesin in *Creem*: "Adrift and singularly unattractive without Wobble's resonant bass, 'Flowers Of Romance' is a collection of nine skeletal cartoons and meandering notions of a possibly sinister, certainly unpleasant nature from a very cocky pop refugee turned art snob suffering from a lethal overdose of UK attention."

The majority of reviews were essentially negative. Of course in the eternal quest to be different, the generally hostile *Sounds* gave the album five stars and printed such comments as, "This is the album mankind has been waiting for: Absolute Music!" However the more balanced reviews came from the likes of the *Sunday Times* ("This album is patently not an avant-garde masterpiece; nor, however, is it self-indulgent nonsense"), the Irish music paper *Hot Press* ("The best bits? They're good, but after this the most subversive thing PiL could do might just turn out to be producing something utterly ordinary") and *New*

Musical Express where Ian Penman's full-page review voiced general fears at the direction Lydon and Levene were pursuing and the pretensions they were assuming along the way. His initial enthusiasm for the four tracks he heard back in December had been tempered by further listenings, but also by the importance that the PiL corporation now seemed to attach to everything it was doing:

"'Flowers Of Romance' is not a collection of film soundtracks – nor does it manipulate its graphic projection in a sufficiently ground-breaking manner to make this anything other than The New PiL LP, complete with Single Off The LP and interviews galore. PiL seem to be so retentively, forlornly hung up – to a blinding, neurotic degree – on their 'anti rock 'n' roll' crusade as to lose sight of where this crusade might actually be taking them."

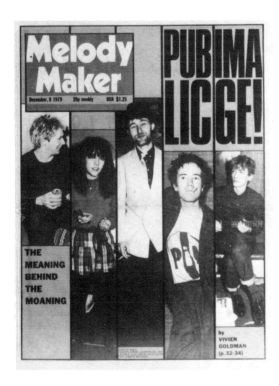

CHAPTER 8

'The (PiL) shareholders are all drunk and the directors as dissolute a bunch of ruffians as I have ever encountered'

Lydon and Levene had already set themselves up for a fall. The repeated references to 'other projects' had come to naught. As Penman pointed out, "In one breath Keith Levene scorns the idea of making an LP as being 'really boring' – then proceeds to bore you for about half an hour (or an entire PiL LP) about the ins and outs of one particular synthesizer technique."

The band's own frustrations at their inability to produce these alternative projects spilled over into repeated 'bleatings' during the (now statutory) bout of interviews to promote The New PiL LP.

Levene simply stated, "We're sick to death of talking about these other projects. We just want to do them. But the problem with that is time, money and people." However Lydon still unashamedly talked of PiL, "as a limited company . . . (who) have access to other things, like video and electronics, and hi-fi and books and painting and yes . . . even the theatre," though even he was prepared to admit that they had "piss-arsed about for far too long. It's more than fucking high time things got serious."

Indicative of perhaps a (temporary) change in attitude was the removal of another (extraneous) member of the corporation, Dave Crowe. When asked what had happened to Crowe, who left the organisation prior to the recording of 'Flowers Of Romance', Levene said: "John had known him for years, so like any excuse would do to get him in the band, so we made him a secretary and he ended up kind of keeping accounts and receipts together and so on. But the PiL thing is that each person must take initiative and must have ideas and just go about them, not like the way Wobble did in a mercenary way, using the company, y'know. Crowe ended up wanting to be told what his job was, and . . . he was creating a lot of head problems, which weren't there."

If Crowe's role had always been ephemeral, Jeanette Lee's role was allegedly far more important. It was her responsibility to expand the visual concepts of the band, though this role was never rigidly defined. It apparently revolved around 'being Jeanette'. She informed Gavin Martin, "I'm always present at studio mixes, and just the fact that I'm there means I'm contributing to the clash of personalities." However under her direction the band even stopped making conventional promotional videos (such as those previously made for 'Public Image' and 'Death Disco').

One project which had seemed more definite than most PiL projects had now fizzled out – the soundtrack for Michael Wadleigh's film about wolves and Indians: "Originally Wadleigh had wanted us to write music to suit the atmosphere . . . about wolves and killing people and that suited us fine of course." Unfortunately it wasn't only PiL who had troubles with finance and the film itself failed to get off the ground, with the musical results (if any) unknown.

With 'Flowers Of Romance' completed, released, charted and its promotion complete, Levene headed for New York and a possible new base of operations. Though PiL had made many mistakes and taken many wrong turns the period to the end of 1980 had not been unproductive. Though 'Flowers Of Romance' was not the direction many supporters of the band wanted them to pursue, at least Lydon and Levene were still coming up with new ideas about the sounds they wanted to produce.

The PiL corporation occasionally became far too embroiled in fruitless projects which had little or no hope of success, and which only served to distract them from the main purpose – making music. In the early months of 1981 this practice now finally started to run unchecked – to the exclusion of all musical endeavours. In a glorious parody of the band's occasional pretensions, the Irish music paper Hot Press published the opinion of the eminent Baron Seamus Of Marzipan on the history of the corporation:

"The firm of Public Image Limited was founded a wee while ago. Its authorised capital is not much, its shareholders are all drunk and the directors as dissolute a bunch of ruffians as I have ever encountered in a Watney's household . . . (The) charge is one of inconsistency, to wit, a lot said but a little achieved, activities likely to enrage and annoy revealing a lack of sympathy for the

The Flowers of Romance

Public Image. Ltd.

a new long playing record.

general populace and sheer bad manners."

In fact any previous "activities likely to enrage and annoy", paled alongside their next public appearance in New York, their first in 12 months, at Manhattan's well-known Ritz club on May 15.

Tom Snyder: "When you perform a live gig do you bring musical instruments to it?"
John Lydon: "So far." *Tomorrow Show* June 1980.

The whole affair started when Bow Wow Wow were forced to cancel their scheduled two-night engagement at the Ritz (due apparently to visa and work permit difficulties). The Ritz offered PiL the cancelled dates while they were over for assorted promotional interviews, and weighing up the possibility of relocating the PiL corporation to New York. It seems that Lydon in particular had grown tired of the harassment and public attention he constantly received 'the other side of the pond' and Levene hoped that New York would be more receptive to the assorted projects he wished to pursue, such as designing his drum synthesizer and building a porta-studio.

In fact Levene later indicated that it was on the day of the Ritz show that he and Lydon had their first major disagreement within PiL. "I originally popped over here for a week; then I got John and Jeanette over here for this thing we really wanted to do, which was a live video gig at the Ritz. All I got from them was that I was treating them like puppets; the morning of the gig they had their suitcases packed, ready to go home. I said, 'Look, fuckin' go home, I don't really care, 'cos if we don't do this gig we'll fuckin' get our legs broken' . . . "

Prior to the show Jeanette Lee talked to journalist Tim Sommer and emphasised, "I hope no one's been misled – no one said it was a gig. Everything is actually going to be done live – there's no preparation. The band will be live, the video will be live – it's all spontaneous. It (organising the gig) happened so quickly, and I'm interested in what we can do in a day – that's the exciting part. The whole thing about this Corporation is spontaneity."

Clearly PiL had improvisation in mind all along. They told the booking agent for the Ritz something of their intentions since he described what

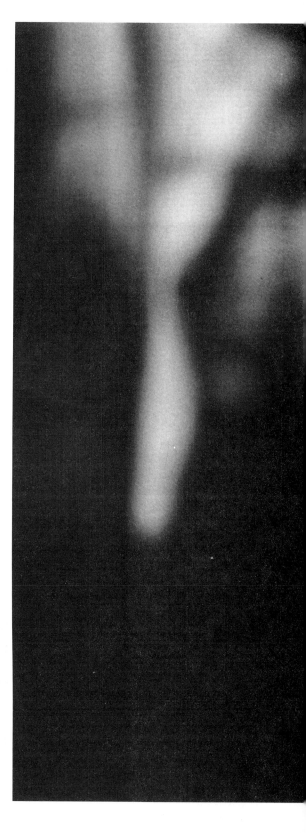

October 26, 1983 Press Conference.

was going to happen as, "art . . . sound and vision". Unfortunately no one told the fans outside what was going to happen. As Sommer later wrote, "Not to warn the audience that this was not going to be a gig, but a video and noise presentation . . . was a major show of gross negligence on the Ritz's part and gross arrogance on PiL's part."

Inside the Ritz ballroom was a large screen that covered the stage but was usually rolled up to the ceiling while bands performed. Instead PiL arrived behind the screen and it was from this position that they began to play.

"A massive array of lights and spots situated behind PiL . . . throw their silhouettes on to the screen – the closer PiL are to the screen, the more defined the silhouette. The video cameras . . . project whatever it is PiL are doing back there on to the huge screen and over the silhouettes." 'Day Of The Locust' *Sounds* May 1981.

"A video camera, also behind the screen, picked up their image which was simultaneously projected on to the screen. Levene stood at his synthesizer, Lydon sang sporadically and Jeanette Lee just wandered around. This simultaneous projection was intercut with old PiL promotional videos, the band in a rehearsal studio, etc." 'Riot At The Ritz' *NME* May 1981.

The band had recruited a drummer and were aiming to provide some degree of live performance – albeit from behind the screen and with video sequences (presumably organised by Jeannette Lee) intercut with shots of themselves. Opening with 'Flowers Of Romance' (pre-recorded), Levene then indulged in assorted synthesizer doodlings while the video screen flickered.

At this early stage the audience were uncertain what the band had in mind and remained reserved in their response. Finally Levene's discernible guitar sound came from the speakers accompanied by drumming and further synthesizers – cut in with the start of the 'Tomorrow Show' on the video screen. The noise from behind the screen finally segued into a discernibly live version of 'Four Enclosed Walls'. All the while the band remained behind the screen on which their im-

ages were 'cut-up' with video inserts.

At this point the audience realised the band were not coming out from behind the screen. And as Richard Grabel's report stated, "The Ritz on a Friday night, it should be said, usually gets a hardcore rock 'n' roll crowd. They expect to be catered to for their 12 dollars and they usually are. The subtleties of a conceptual video performance, or whatever it was PiL thought they were doing, were bound to be lost on them."

Accordingly Lydon started taunting the crowd, with inevitable results:

Lydon: "Hello. So glad you're enjoying the show. That's right, get your money's worth. (background synthesizer noises) . . . (audience boos)) . . . Boo! Boo! It's not fair. It's not fair. We want rock 'n' roll. Boo! Hiss! (sings in high-pitched whine), 'When the sun comes shining through/ just for youuu . . . ' All financial donations accepted. Oh you're so wonderful. So nice to be here in your wonderful city y'know (starts 'Go Back', quickly grinds to a halt amid assorted cries of "Fuck You") . . . Was I wonderful? Aren't you getting your money's worth? This is what rock 'n' roll's all about, maaaan. I'm so happy, so happy you've all come to see me. Ah I'm having so much fun. Would you like to know who's behind the screen? All right here's Sammy on drums. Well hello Sammy, how you doing? Isn't it pretty groovy? Now this is Keith Levene, you've heard of him – he's pretty famous. And now over here we have Jeanette Lee. Hi there, Jeanette, say hello to the guys and girls. ("Hello guys and girls") There, getting your money's worth. Go Back."

Bottles now started raining on the screen. Levene further incited the crowd, "I think you're boring. You're a boring fucking audience. If you destroy that fucking screen we will destroy you. We have the power behind us. If you destroy the screen you are destroyed." (Lydon starts reciting 'Go Back' and the music starts up again.)

Lydon: "I'm safe . . . You're not throwing enough. You're what I call a passive audience. It's obvious you're all into peace and love . . . Hey I can see you're having fun out there." (Assorted shouts of "Fuck You", Lydon starts singing re-

Punk meets punk – Linda Davidson of Eastenders and Johnny Rotten
– at launch of Smith and Jones book – London, '86.

peatedly in high-pitched whine). 'Happiness, Happiness/ The greatest gift that I possess . . . Video killed the radio star/ Video killed the audience again. Kill the fucking audience . . . ' I'm so glad you're all into new ideas. Destroy! Destroy! Go on – destroy. It's The Sex Pistols all over again. I've seen it all before. (Sings in high-pitched whine) 'New York New York/Is a wonderful town'.''

"At 1.50 a chair was heaved from the balcony, hitting the screen dead centre and smashing down on the stage. This was the signal for the true riot to begin. Suddenly, Keith darted out from behind the screen, a truly possessed and angry look on his face. Who knows why he decided to appear – he looked set to kill. He made it about 10 feet out from the wings when a bottle swiped him on the forehead and a bouncer grabbed Levene and tossed him back behind the screen, quite literally saving his life." 'Day Of The Locust' *Sounds*.

At this point the band quit the stage as the audience grabbed the screen and pulled it down, amidst shouts of "Smash the fucking lens", the inevitable "Fuck you" and "Play some fucking music". The perennial New York fights between fans and bouncers broke out as the stage was covered with the broken glass from the bottles the fans had been throwing at the screen; and the affair "ended with the block on which the club is located being sealed off by police, a mob of angry people gathered outside the doors, several injuries and thousands of dollars worth of damage done inside the club."

Warner Brothers promptly organised a press conference on the Tuesday of the following week at which PiL could explain their performance. Instead Levene showed the attendant press a video of the show, which the band had indeed filmed, "I am satisfied it had impact and we'll do it again but it'll be altogether different," he said.

Levene was clearly more than happy with the performance, and later stated (in 1983): "(In fact) everyone I spoke to said it was brilliant. The American public, I hear, thinks it was some kind of rip off; I'm sure I would have found that gig worth my 10 dollars. The idea that we weren't really gonna know what was going to happen. As you saw we didn't. We weren't trying to start a riot . . . that was the last thing we were trying to do. We had a boom mike over the audience I wanted this communication between the audience."

Lydon, on the other hand, was dismissive of both the audience and anybody who sought to see some great artistic conceit in the events at the Ritz on May 15: "They wanted some kind of rock 'n' roll band. Pity, 'cos that's not what they are going to get from us. Piss off to them, they have a pretty good idea what to expect next time we do a gig . . . I would not knowingly ever play to an 'Art' crowd. I hate arteests."

CHAPTER 9

'I find it bloody irritating that people pay more attention to the sociological phenomenon of PiL than the music we play'

"On Friday, May 15, PiL performed at the Ritz nightclub in New York and obliterated those boundaries between theatre and real life, between the mock violence and the implied threat of the Dead Kennedys ... and the real desire of an audience to destroy a band and everything they stood for ... It is also the first time that PiL has actually done what they've always said they were going to do, actually lived up to and acted on everything they claim to stand for and have stated that they wanted to achieve." 'Day Of The Locust' *Sounds*.

Unbeknown to the band the Ritz gig had considerably limited their options. Having left England and Virgin behind, their gesture at The Ritz now left them without the prospect of playing any live shows in the States. It also confirmed the band's status as *enfants terrible*, and as such something to be avoided rather than covered by the US media.

Though the gig was undoubtedly an audacious experiment, like the 'Flowers Of Romance' album, it placed them outside boundaries that media and record companies could deal with. Rather than being different, as 'Metal Box' presented them to be, they were seen as dangerous, fundamentally concerned with overthrowing the order of things. This was a laudable (and marketable) virtue only if the threat was not perceived as real or serious.

Ironically the one offer of help made in the aftermath of the riot came from the management of The Ritz who, "perhaps finding the publicity from the fray outweighs the cost incurred by the audience throwing bottles and trashing the video screen, are offering PiL large sums of money for a return, though probably not a repeat, perform-ance." The offer was not taken up and it would be a further 16 months before anything more would be heard from the PiL corporation. As the percep-tive reviewer in *Hot Press* wrote of 'Flowers Of Romance': "After this the most subversive thing PiL could do might just turn out to be producing something utterly ordinary."

There followed a year of crashing silence from PiL, broken only by the occasional worrying rumour, such as one printed in *Sounds* in January 1982 that the band had 'disintegrated'. Lydon's response was, "The tosspot was desperate for a story last week, so he made one up." In fact PiL had apparently co-opted another long-standing acquaintance into the band – Ken Lockie, listed as keyboardist. Meanwhile Virgin claimed the band's failure to produce any product from their New York sojourn was down to, "the unavailability of certain new innovative synthesized and other electro-music technology."

In fact it would be the Spring of 1982 before PiL showed signs of rising from their self-imposed torpor. What occurred was fairly indicative of the slothful streak in Lydon which had previously been held in some kind of check. According to Patrick Zerbib in his remarkable exposé of the decline of John Lydon in the December 1983 edition of *The Face*:

"For the first few months in New York, PiL lived very well thanks to an advance from Virgin Records on their next album. After all, 'Metal Box' hadn't done so badly; nearly 50,000 copies worldwide. The group installed themselves in a luxury hotel. A star in America must act like one. But the dollars soon disappeared and PiL fled to the Chelsea Hotel, infamous refuge of bankrupt stars. As well as John, there was ... Keith Levene and Jeanette Lee, in charge of the group's videos, posters, sleeves."

So what did the band do during these months. Tim Sommer's report, 'Public Enterprises', in an October 1982 edition of *Sounds*, spelled out what had happened:

"PiL did absolutely nothing as a band but drink beer and watch videos and hang out, any co-hesiveness about the PiL unit/concept dissolved in a lazy haze. John put on weight, Keith (to some, but admittedly not to all) became an intolerable star/junkie, Jeanette Lee maintained the public profile of the so-called band, and the Lydon personality cult drew leeches and starfuckers like any personality cult would, some like Ken Lockie masking their groupie-ism with musicianship, others, like Roger Trilling and Bob Tullipan, mask-ing it with 'management'."

Indeed according to Zerbib, Lydon now,

"preferred to pass the time in bed watching quiz shows on the TV while working his way through 15 cans of beer a day." Not that this was anything new. In the winter of 1981 Lydon had provided a diary of a week in the life of John Lydon for *Smash Hits*, which included such revealing snippets as "Stayed around at Nora's . . . had a long video session," "The only day I left the house. I went to the off-licence . . . That's all I did," and "I spent the rest of the day watching the telly. I'm a TV addict."

However Lydon's slothful inclinations were probably exacerbated by his increasing sense of isolation (save for the occasional ego-massaging exercise offered by hangers-on). One of the results of all this inactivity was that PiL's American label, Warner Brothers, gave them the proverbial boot, seeing "PiL for the unproductive moneywasters they were."

When it seemed that PiL as a creative unit was well and truly finished a chance meeting between Levene and Martin Atkins at the Mudd Club in New York provided some impetus for a rekindling of PiL activities. Atkins was playing the club with his band Brian Brain, and Levene "invited him to stick around and work on a new PiL record."

In fact Levene had already come across two lawyers who wanted to help the group and owned a small recording studio, South Park Studios. They offered the band studio-time, and requested only minimal cash payment upfront. Nevertheless even a minimal upfront payment could have proved problematic if Lydon had not accepted an acting role by Italian director Roberto Faenza in his new movie.

The movie, initially entitled *Psycho Jogger*, was to be shot in New York's Central Park and in Rome, and Lydon was offered a measly (but highly welcome) $10,000 to appear in it – as a psycho-jogging cop killer. As such Lydon was required to play pretty much himself! Filming was due to start at the beginning of May and initially it was suggested that PiL would provide the soundtrack music for the film, though this did not in fact prove to be the case.

The net result of this bout of activity was that, "Keith and Martin spent the late spring and summer in the studio, usually in crazy 24 hours," while Lydon was holed up in Rome. En route to New York from Rome, Lydon spent a few days in London in late July during which he talked with a curious *NME* editor, Neil Spencer, about what had happened to John Lydon and PiL. He was quite open about what had happened to John Lydon: "I'll tell you what I did in New York for a year . . . sat and watched American TV. And I loved it."

As to what PiL were up to: "It's been difficult because I've been away two-and-a-half months and that's a long time to be separated. Keith's been at work because we have a very good studio deal with some people we might be amalgamating with. He's been banging down rough ideas and I've been sending over lyrics."

PiL were also putting their business matters on a sounder footing, setting up their own record label – P.E.P. – Public Entertainment Productions and also an organisation called M.I.C. (Multi Image Corporation), which according to Levene was intended as, "an expansion of the original PiL idea, but it's not a group whatsoever. It facilitates a multitude of people going in a multitude of directions. It also produces PiL's music and co-ordinates PiL's artwork." By November 1982 a six-track mini-album, 'You Are Now Entering A Commercial Zone', was apparently ready for release. Accordingly the band announced a West Coast press conference to be held at glitzy Hollywood restaurant Le Dome to announce new plans and a return to gigging.

At the press conference Lydon was at pains to insist that PiL were not an 'arty' band – all their music was designed to be accessible: "I find it bloody irritating that people pay more attention to the 'sociological phenomenon' of Public Image than the music we play."

At the same time – following the departure of Jeanette Lee – the band abandoned some of their illusions of grander designs. The exact reasons/timing of her departure are not clear. Even Levene confessed, "I don't know what happened between her and John when he went to Italy with her to make the movie, but she left after that. Who knows, who cares?" In fact she was still with

1982/3 live: Levene and Lydon.

Lydon when he was interviewed by Neil Spencer in London in July, so it may well be that she took the opportunity to stay in London, rather than face the continuing uncertainty of operations in New York.

Meanwhile Martin Atkins had drafted in a new bass player, a fellow member of Brian Brain, Pete Jones, though it was probably still Keith Levene who continued to record the majority of bass parts in the studio. However it did mean that for the first time in over two years, in fact since Wobble's departure, the band were able to resume gigging – maybe not along the lines of such minimalist exercises as the Ritz debacle – but more worthwhile, profitable and straightforward affairs.

One member of the band also had new responsibilities in the form of Mrs Lori Levene, who married Keith in November. Undoubtedly this union, to an American girl, helped stabilise Levene's occasional excesses. However it also

sowed the seeds of the band's ultimate demise as a creative force. As Levene admitted in 1983: "My marriage had a great deal to do with me leaving PiL, it was an integral reason. The way my wife puts it – which doesn't make me look too great – is that I was with a lot of bastards that were giving me a hard time and I was too much a nice guy to know it."

The band rehearsed some new material for a series of dates – which commenced in New York on September 28, 1982. Not so much a 'tour' as a casual saunter across the States (with New York remaining as base), PiL played around a dozen shows over some two months, including four shows on the West Coast at the beginning of November. They seem to have concluded their stint across America with a show in Atlanta on December 11.

At the shows the band premièred three new songs, though the first show in New York only featured (two parts of) one new song: 'Lou Reed

Part One' and 'Where Are You (Lou Reed Part Two)'. Later introduced were two more songs: 'Blue Water' (which was scheduled to be the next PiL single) and 'Mad Max' (subsequently rechristened 'Bad Life').

The greatest surprise however, was just how mainstream both the shows and the new songs were. It was as if the band had wholly written off the two years since Wobble's departure as an unsuccessful sideturn, and returned to their original direction. 'Where Are You' in particular was a song which would have fitted perfectly comfortably on either of the first two albums, while 'Blue Water' and 'Mad Max' showed a more discreet (and successful) flirtation with synthesizers than anything on 'Flowers Of Romance'.

The shows were also successful, if nonconfrontational, affairs. Only one song was being featured from 'Flowers Of Romance' – 'Under The House' – and on the first night at New York's Roseland Ballroom, Lydon even allowed a second version of 'Public Image' as an encore. That show started with an instrumental 'Lou Reed Part One' and 'Where Are You (Lou Reed Part Two)', so Lydon's opening line at the gig was 'Hello, hello' – almost as if about to launch into 'Public Image' – but instead performing 'Where Are You', which finally segued into an ecstatically-received 'Public Image'. The set featured five songs from the first album, though only two from 'Metal Box' ('Death Disco' and 'Chant').

The equilibrium between PiL's two major albums was later restored with 'Bad Baby', 'Careering' and 'No Birds Do Sing' though at one show (at The Elite Club in California) PiL actually performed all of the first album with the exception of 'Fodderstompf', along with five songs from 'Metal Box' and three new songs. By PiL standards this 14-song set was a mammoth show.

Of course the band had placed themselves in a no-win situation: if they played a conventional gig they would be criticised for a lack of innovation; if they tried experiments like the Ritz they would be castigated as anarchists and trouble-makers. Both David Fricke's and Richard Grabel's reviews of the New York show considered it a chanceless affair, Fricke concluding, "the safety factor of familiar material and the concentrated vigour with which they play it suggests PiL feel the need to redeem themselves as an active, battling unit," whilst Grabel's slightly sour review ended with, "PiL put on a good show and perhaps it's sour grapes not to leave it at that. But they are too sharp to rest on their laurels, and good as it was, this show was just coasting."

However the most baffling aspect of all this activity was the lack of even a single to promote. The band had presumably already recorded the studio versions of the songs they were performing in concert, plus probably at least two further instrumentals, 'Miller High Life' and 'The Slab' (later rechristened 'Order Of Death') and 'Bad Night', a vocal track not subsequently performed in concert or included on the post-Levene album, 'This Is What You Want, This Is What You Get' (though it appears along with the remaining songs from this period on 'Commercial Zone – Limited Edition').

Possibly the band had abandoned the idea of a mini-album and continued to record further material for a full album-length follow-up to 'Flowers Of Romance'. Two songs which almost certainly date from the late winter or early spring of 1983 are 'This Is Not A Love Song' and 'Solitaire'. With these songs an album was finally completed and ready for release – over two years after 'Flowers Of Romance' was completed. Yet it would be a further year before the album 'Commercial Zone' was released.

CHAPTER 10

'There's an awful lot of weak people in the world'

While PiL completed the long-awaited follow-up to 'Flowers Of Romance', they organised occasional gigs in New York and New Jersey, playing Long Beach on New Year's Eve, the Brooklyn Zoo in January and Poughkeepsie and Staten Island in March – the last PiL gigs to feature Keith Levene and in effect the end of the band that had formed back in 1978. According to Levene these gigs were as disorganised as ever: "We charged as much as possible, but because we were so disorganised we spent just as much hiring the equipment and getting there."

Relations between Lydon and Levene were deteriorating and the completion of 'Commercial Zone' and mixing of 'This Is Not A Love Song', now scheduled as the band's next single, proved to be Levene's last acts with PiL. The final split came over the mixing of a song to achieve a particular sound, originally such a binding factor between Levene and Lydon (and indeed Wobble).

All that remains from this line-up is the album 'Commercial Zone – Limited Edition', an album Lydon would not sanction for release, even though Levene made it clear in November 1983 that . . . "The record is finished – I finished it. I guess that was against PiL's will, but they weren't doing anything about it . . . Personally, if I was John Lydon, I wouldn't have said the vocals were finished, but they said they were. I went in and made the best of a bad job. But the album turned out quite good."

In fact the album did eventually reach the shops though in a surreptitious manner. It initially appeared in the winter of 1984 as a small pressing in the US, with a blank sleeve, a poor facsimile of the PiL logo on the label, and with 'This Is Not A Love Song' opening the album. It was then issued as a *bona fide* release and more widely distributed, shortly after the release of 'This Is What You Want . . .', this time opening with 'Mad Max'. It was therefore in direct competition with Lydon's re-recorded (and vastly inferior) versions of the same material featured on the official Virgin release.

It is sad to consider that if 'Commercial Zone' had been released in the spring of 1983, it might

well have reversed the band's fortunes. 'Commercial Zone', though like 'First Issue' short on time (it clocks in at just over 32 minutes, of which over 10 minutes are taken up with the three instrumentals), is the last of PiL's trio of classic albums: as commercial as the second side of 'First Issue' but with the marvellous sparsity of sound that graced 'Metal Box'. In fact this version of 'Mad Max' would have made as good (and probably as successful) a single as 'This Is Not A Love Song'; and the three instrumentals prove that PiL would have made some fine film soundtracks if they had been given the opportunity. Possibly these three songs originated from the Spring 1982 sessions intended to provide the soundtrack for *Order Of Death*.

Instead 'Commercial Zone' languished in a vault while Lydon issued a non-authentic live album under the name of PiL and, having secured considerable commercial success with a single of 'This Is Not A Love Song' (featuring Levene), issued inferior re-recordings of 'Bad Life' (aka 'Mad Max'), 'Solitaire', 'Where Are You', 'This Is Not A Love Song' and 'Order Of Death' minus Levene – all of which were singularly unsuccessful.

Actually Levene's departure from the band does not seem to have been simply the result of one particular incident but rather a general disillusionment with what the band had become: "The last six to eight months we were going around being everything we always swore we would never want to be. I was aware of it. I had to see the scene through, but I had to say goodbye in the end. I never said, I quit. I told Martin, 'You do know, don't you, that I'm not going to Japan with you and I don't want to work with you again, or see you again?'"

However the catalyst for Levene's departure was certainly one particular telephone call from Lydon in Los Angeles. Levene had increasingly grown to despise Atkins' 'buddy-buddy' act with Lydon, for it was Atkins who seemed intent on driving a wedge between Levene and Lydon: "John was in LA by then . . . I went into the studio to remix 'Love Song'. I told them I've got to remix

it, it is embarrassing. Martin called John in LA and told him I was in the studio – this was the major trump card in Martin's power play to be John's best buddy. John called up screaming that I should get out of the studio immediately."

Lydon went to Los Angeles at the instigation of one Larry White, sometime sound engineer, sometime road manager and general entrepreneur. He apparently told Lydon, "You'll never make it with your sound; what a bunch of wankers! The people want to see Johnny Rotten, man. Do you realise what you've got in your hands? Besides, you need a real band."

White introduced Lydon to Westside Frankie And The Inglewood Jerks an obscure band from New Jersey who, "knew The Sex Pistols repertoire by heart." Lydon apparently then rehearsed PiL material with this band and tried out the show at a small club in LA. The show ended with 'Anarchy In The UK'. The fans pogoed away.

Levene heard stories of Lydon's sojourn in LA and was understandably concerned, and when Lydon started screaming at him, "You just get out of the fucking studio or you won't be part of PiL any more," Levene went on the attack: "I don't like what I've been hearing about you in LA. It's a joke! Singing 'Anarchy In The UK' . . . We're doing all the things we said we'd never do. Is that what you want? A sell-out?" Lydon hung up.

"That day, Lydon lost a friend. And not for the first time. One by one, over the years, they had given him up. Because he's a fatalist. Because he believes in nothing, except himself. But he swallows each new loss, and feels stronger." 'Situation Vacant' (*The Face*, December 1983).

Following previous models of PiL departures, there was considerable acrimony on both sides. When Lydon was asked on Melbourne radio in December 1984 where Levene was, he replied, "Dead – I hope." Levene was equally caustic. "I thought he had a unique talent but I don't think he's got it any more . . . John was my best friend for years. I thought he was great, so great. It was me, John and Sid . . . Sid died . . . and John has now died as far as I'm concerned. I don't want the PiL name and I don't want to be associated with

them any more."

Whatever comments Lydon subsequently made about Levene, he would not be drawn on the whole question of PiL's metamorphosis into the John Lydon band. At his October 1983 press conference in London he was asked why Levene and Jeanette Lee had left the group: "They're quitters." So why have there been so many quitters involved in PiL? "There's an awful lot of weak people in the world."

Meanwhile Lydon had been offered an eight-date tour of Japan at the beginning of July, for a fee of $9,000 plus expenses. The offer was too tempting to refuse, especially with Lydon's financial problems, and he returned to New York, with new manager Larry White, to rehearse with Atkins and his new band. Pete Jones left the band a month prior to Levene so Lydon also required a bassist. In Jones' place was Louie Bernardi. Joe Guda replaced Keith Levene on guitar and Lydon introduced a keyboards player to the band for the first time – Tom Zvoncheck. Zvoncheck's role seemed to be to disguise the lack of any distinctive guitar-sound, originally PiL's trademark, along with Wobble's rumbling bass.

The band duly arrived in Japan to play the first of eight shows on June 21. The tour centred wholly around Tokyo where 'PiL' played six concerts at the Nakano Sun Plaza. While there Lydon was offered the opportunity of recording a live album on one of only three Mitsubishi X-800 PCM 32ch digital tape recorders in the world. Two of the last three shows were duly recorded, and also filmed for a possible video release, an ironic gesture considering the band's previous failure to produce a video during PiL's creative years.

The actual material performed by the band was a cross-section of PiL's entire career, including three songs from 'Flowers Of Romance' (the title song, 'Under The House' and 'Banging The Door'), and three songs recorded for 'Commercial Zone' ('This Is Not A Love Song', 'Solitaire' and 'Bad Life' née 'Mad Max'). Also performed, as an encore, was 'Anarchy In The UK'. Thankfully this was not included on the resultant live album.

The Japanese shows ushered in an unpre-

1983 Arthur Stead, Martin Atkins, Joseph Guda, John Lydon, Louie Bernardi.

cedented bout of activity from the band. On September 5, 1983 PiL issued its first record in 29 months which were the last PiL recordings to feature Keith Levene. Using Virgin's 1981 idea (the re-release of 'Public Image'), Lydon issued as a seven-inch, 'This Is Not A Love Song' backed by the first PiL A-side. The 12-inch was somewhat better value, featuring an alternate version of 'This Is Not A Love Song' (possibly the Levene mix which had caused such acrimony), and 'Blue Water' – which had been scheduled to be PiL's comeback single back in 1982.

Despite the long absence, this marvellously exuberant single proved to be PiL's best-selling single ever, reaching number five and staying in the charts for 10 weeks. It was a shrewd, calculating move on Lydon's part to test the water with the unashamedly commercial 'This Is Not A Love Song' before announcing future plans for his return to the UK music scene. It was an equally

shrewd move to release an (albeit sanitized) live greatest hits album – featuring the new hit single – on the heels of the single's success.

'Live In Tokyo' hit the shops three weeks after the release of the single, and a week after the single entered the charts. If the music did not exactly exemplify PiL's previous achievements, the production did. The album was wondrously recorded. Indeed both Lydon and Atkins maintained that the primary purpose of the album had been simply to use the digital equipment from which the recordings were made.

Atkins told *International Musician*: "The idea of the Japanese album was not so much to freeze the Tokyo gig but to have the opportunity of using hi-tech 32-track Japanese digital equipment. In fact it's the first digital live album that I know of." Virgin even released the album in PiL-like form, as two 12-inch singles, to maintain the hi-fidelity sound of the recording.

Unfortunately the music wasn't worth the effort, and the reviewers were for once universal in their distaste. Particularly curt and to the point was Richard Cook who wrote: "'Tokyo' is Lydon, the entertainer, in ghastly pieces. PiL is now down to him alone. Martin Atkins is back at the drums but his role, like that of Louie Bernardi, Tom Zvoncheck and Joseph Guida, is merely to perform charts. PiL's sound has become as formal and inelastic as elevator music: it is, again, noise – without heart or flesh of any sort."

Despite such reviews the album was a much greater success than 'Paris Au Printemps', cracking the Top 30 and remaining in the charts for six weeks, galvanised first by the success of the single and then by the announcement of PiL's first UK tour – to commence at the beginning of November and, according to *Sounds*, "Their first appearances here since a show at London's Rainbow on Christmas Day 1978." To further promote the tour, which would venture into mainland Europe at the end of November before returning to the UK for further shows in December, PiL appeared on Channel 4's *The Tube* on October 28, five days before the opening show in Brighton.

Unfortunately Lydon gave the game away on nationwide TV by performing an unutterably awful version of 'Anarchy In The UK' sandwiched between PiL's last two singles. It was a profound disappointment to those who still hoped that, "crossing over to the other side" did not mean Lydon forsaking PiL's previous ideals. In particular the blandness of the band, partially disguised by the sheer quality of the Tokyo recording, was truly brought into sharp focus.

Lydon later insisted that the whole affair was one of his famous 'wind-ups': "It was just about the most appalling bad taste thing to do . . . a cocktail jazz outfit behind me struck me as being mighty wicked and funny . . . I did enjoy it! It was just about the worst thing that a human being could be capable of. It was spiteful and malicious, yes, but it was funny."

The previous day he granted a press conference, à la Bowie, to announce the tour and release of his new movie, *Order Of Death*, on November 3. This experience should have provided Lydon with a reasonable indication of how badly members of the music press took his desertion of PiL's previous ideals. But if some journalists were determined to discomfort Lydon, or preferably get him to explain the effective dissolution of PiL, there was another type of journalist attending, as Neil Spencer explained.

"For most of Fleet Street this is their first re-encounter with Lydon since Pistol trading days, and they're curious because they always did wonder what happened to Johnny Rotten and they never could understand what the hell that weird music he made after the Pistols split up was all about."

The music journalists had little chance to strike back at Lydon's nicely-rehearsed repartee at the press conference, though they extracted suitable revenge in a series of some of the most scathing gig reviews dished out to any band since, well, since PiL played the Rainbow in 1978.

The comments in the music press suggested that they took it very personally that Johnny had taken them all for a ride: "(You have) become the complete antithesis of everything you once stood for, wallowing in the star-trip whilst simultaneously sending it up."

"Whatever his charm this man is redundant."

"When PiL started they were a band, now they're Lydon and a backing group. I remember Lydon complaining when morons shouted for 'Anarchy In The UK' at the Futurama – now they are fucking playing it."

In most cases the band came in for as much if not more stick than Lydon:

"Johnny's cast of robots jog onto the stage."

"The appalling *Play Away* trained backing band . . . (are) proficient and dull."

"Joe, Chuck, Dirk and (of course) Martin Atkins slip frighteningly efficiently into . . . a lack-lustre 'Death Disco'."

One effect of the tour was to undo the groundwork that the superb 'This Is Not A Love Song' had done. PiL's commercialism was once again thrown into question.

CHAPTER 11

*'I've got everything I need in Los Angeles.
Fifty TV channels'*

Lydon decided not to release 'Commercial Zone', but to re-record the material in England after the tour, with only Martin Atkins in tow. Most of the sessions were held at Maison Rouge Studios in south west London. He also chose not to follow-up 'This Is Not A Love Song' with a further recording from the New York sessions, the supremely funky 'Bad Life'. Instead he decided to issue a new studio version of the song. The effect of this was to delay the follow-up to PiL's best-selling single until May 1984, when everyone had forgotten 'This Is Not A Love Song'; and also to release a version of the single decidedly less commercial than the original. The single was a miserable failure, peaking at a none-too-impressive 71, and sliding out of the Top 100 in two weeks flat.

It was also a most unwelcome non-advertisement for the first studio album in PiL's name for some three years. PiL's fourth studio album, appropriately entitled 'This Is What You Want, This Is What You Get', was issued in July to universally scathing reviews. Aside from five songs from 'Commercial Zone' (badly re-recorded) the album also featured three Lydon-Atkins compositions of no determinate worth. A fourth Lydon-Atkins piece of nonsense ('Question Mark') filled up the B-side of 'Bad Life' and provided a fair forewarning of things to come.

Lydon later claimed that . . . "There was some legal nonsense with a studio bill, so some tracks had to be redone in a hurry." However if he was referring to the 'Commercial Zone' material, this hardly explains how two songs from those sessions had already been released on single; nor why releasing the new versions a year later was redoing them "in a hurry"; nor why Virgin should not pay an old studio bill in preference to incurring a new bill; nor indeed Levene's virtually concurrent commercial release of 'Commercial Zone – Limited Edition'.

Levene revelled in the opportunity to compare his release with Lydon's: "I was waiting for the other record to be released, and now that has come out . . . anyone who's ever been into PiL can now get hold of the record and make their own

comparisons . . . 'Commercial Zone' is the real alternative to the Virgin effort as it's more in the vein of what PiL was all about – the new PiL album as opposed to the new PiL image, the real members, not the 'Holiday Inn' substitute."

Without a tour, hit single, or bout of promotional interviews to help sell the album, 'This Is What You Want . . .' was a commercial disaster. It peaked at 56, and remained in the charts for two weeks – PiL's greatest commercial disaster and a fair indication that Lydon was no longer either a commercial or creative force to be reckoned with.

However his previous achievements were enough to secure PiL bookings in other far-flung places in the world. Consequently another PiL line-up – still featuring Atkins – toured the States in the autumn and in December 1984 played their first shows in Australia. Still playing 'Anarchy In The UK', Lydon was also now singing 'Bodies' from The Pistols' repertoire – plus two of the three Lydon-Atkins compositions on the last album, '1981' and 'Tie Me To The Lamp-post', though neither was particularly improved in concert.

Thankfully Atkins, whose demeanour towards Lydon in a Melbourne radio interview late that month had long since crossed the boundaries of sycophancy, was on the way out and Lydon was at least preparing to look out of the pit into which he had dug himself.

Lydon had always required someone else to 'bounce ideas off', preferably also to provide the technical expertise (and generally the tunes) that he lacked himself. In the early days of The Pistols it had been Glen Matlock, later Steve Jones. In the early PiL it had been Wobble and Levene, finally it was just Levene. In all cases Lydon had selected and associated with individuals of considerable creative ability. However in the case of Martin Atkins, Lydon was associating with a figure of less (if any) ability and minimal musical sensibilities. Lydon also required someone to stand up against him, and neither Larry White – his personal manager through 1983/4 – nor Atkins were likely to tell Lydon when he was producing substandard rubbish either on stage or in the studio.

After the disastrous 'This Is What You Want,

Atkins, Lydon, Bernardi.

This Is What You Get', Lydon required the impetus another quality musician could provide. The first result of a necessary rethink by Lydon was released on New Year's Eve 1984 and was of all things a rap record. Lydon joined up with Afrika Bambaataa to produce a single called 'World Destruction' under the joint moniker Time Zone.

The sound of the single had the sledgehammer power of early PiL recordings, even if it was really a very straightforward piece of rapping and Lydon seems to have enjoyed the whole experience of making a rap record (though Bambaataa's contribution certainly sounds the greater). However perhaps even more impressive than the single was the video Lydon and Bambaataa produced, a most effective collage of TV screens spouting 'World Destruction' (the song opens with Reagan 'discussing' Armageddon), animation and Lydon smearing his face in ketchup and grimacing at the camera whilst Bambaataa cruises the streets.

The Time Zone single also introduced Lydon to his most worthwhile post-Levene collaborator, Bill Laswell, the producer of 'World Destruction'. Laswell had a reputation for his production of black artists. According to Lydon the opportunity to work with Laswell was a main reason for recording the song, "It was my first chance to work with Bill in the studio, and I'd had him in mind as someone to use in a producer capacity for years . . . Me and Laswell used that record to test each other out. He wasn't sure whether or not I was a silly ignorant punk rocker, or someone who really knew what he was talking about."

It was Laswell who also convinced Lydon to contribute to the second album by The Golden Palominos, a band/ensemble of perennially changing membership devised by Anton Fier (though with some help from Laswell). On this second album, 'Visions Of Excess', Lydon joined some eminent company (the likes of Michael Stipe, Richard Thompson and Jack Bruce), contributing lead vocals on one song, 'The Animal Speaks' written by the mysterious Robert Kidney.

Though the album was produced by Fier, Laswell played bass on all tracks and doubtless had his say in how the album sounded. The sound on 'The Animal Speaks' previewed the best of the material on PiL's next album, a furious heavy sound over-laden with Lydon's famous high-pitched whine. The song starts with an unmistakable belch before noise overwhelms and from then on Lydon struggles to be heard in the morass. The song boded well for a long-term association with Laswell, despite a hint of heavy metal in the sound of the guitars on both 'World Destruction' and 'The Animal Speaks'.

Lydon's brief sojourn in England, from the autumn of 1983 through the first half of 1984, was now over and he returned to Los Angeles, and set up residence. There he set about reconstructing a new 'PiL' – for something like the fifteenth time. The nucleus of the new band was Jebbin Bruni and Mark Schulz, with whom Lydon also started writing songs. Laswell also continued his association, working on songs with Lydon as well.

Atkins finally left PiL in May 1985.

For 1985 Lydon stayed holed up in Los Angeles with his long-standing paramour, Nora Foster, mother of Ari-Up of The Slits. Indeed at some point in 1985 he finally married Nora, who was nigh on 20 years his senior. He was happier away from the home of punk: "PiL as PiL are popular in America now and people come for PiL, not for The Sex Pistols."

When Lydon did decide to return to the studio to record PiL's fifth studio album, it was with Laswell as co-producer and bassist. However he did not enter the studio with Bruni and Schulz – despite four of the seven songs on the album being co-written with them: "I had a live band before recording took place and a lot of material together before going into the studio, but the band was totally inexperienced. They would have put the budget up by an incredible amount so we decided to use session people – and why not get the best available?"

The band Lydon and Laswell put together featured Steve Vai (for "his stuff with Zappa"), Ginger Baker ("a bloody good drummer and always has been to my mind") and Riuchi Sakamoto (for his "eclectic jazz keyboard angle"). Unfortunately Lydon also told Laswell, "I want to do a rock album." It would appear the slow descent back to the mainstream was continuing.

The release of the pre-album single however seemed to belie this theory. 'Rise' appeared to confirm the mini-renaissance hinted at by 'World Destruction' and 'The Animal Speaks'. The single was released in January 1986 and was instantly acclaimed as one of the great PiL singles, which indeed it was. The guitar riff was a jangling reminder of the ghost of Levene, and the drumming would not have been out of place on 'Flowers Of Romance'. The lyrics were also a return to form, not-to-say pertinence ("I read this manual on South African interrogation techniques and 'Rise' is quotes from some of the victims."):

'They put a hot wire to my head/ 'Cause of the things I did and said.'

Even the production of the single was splendid,

and 'Rise' proved a most popular 45, peaking at number 11 and remaining in the charts for eight weeks, PiL's third best selling single (behind 'Public Image' and 'This Is Not A Love Song'). Lydon commissioned Hipgnosis to design a uniform packaging for single, album and promotional material. As such 'Single' or '12-inch Single' (rather than 'Rise') introduced the new 'public image'. All in all it proved a most successful exercise in marketing. However the success of 'This Is Not A Love Song' was not capitalised upon with 'Live In Tokyo' or the 1983 tour or 'This Is What You Want . . .'.

Circumstances prompted Lydon to visit

London where he promoted 'Rise' by filming a new video, and at the same time finally resolved his long-standing battle with McLaren over the ownership of The Sex Pistols name and monies. When the case finally reached the High Court in January 1986, Mr Justice Mervyn Davies ruled that the name Sex Pistols was the property of Lydon, Paul Cook, Steve Jones and Sid Vicious' estate. He also awarded them all the monies in receivership (supposedly over a million pounds), and all rights to *The Great Rock 'n' Roll Swindle*, Glitterbest and Matrixbest.

Lydon duly undertook an unprecedented bout of promotional interviews, affording him full opportunity to gloat over his legal and commercial successes. The number of interviews he conducted was far larger than the days when only *Sounds*, *NME* and *MM* would cover Lydon – plus *Zigzag* since they invariably said nice things about the band. Indeed 'overkill' is the word that springs to mind considering the list: *Extra* (a free London paper), *Smash Hits*, *NME*, *i-D*, *Record Mirror*, *Blitz*, *Kerrang!*, *Number One*, *City Limits*, *Sounds* (a two-parter) and of course *Melody Maker* all featuring interviews in their February issues. Vivien Goldman even wrote a profile/interview for a women's magazine. Only *The Face* was excluded, presumably as a 'punishment' for their 1983 attack on Lydon.

The interviews centred wholly on expositions of the good life according to Johnny Rotten: "I've got everything I need in Los Angeles. Fifty TV channels! The sun's outside . . . I hate the sun but it's nice to know it's there . . . I rise at 4.30 in the afternoon. In bed by 12. Watch films all night . . . I absorb culture through my backside."

If there was any question of a return to the idealism of 1978-81, Lydon quickly dispersed it: "I think I talked too much (in the past) and stuck myself in a hole, but at least I'm honest enough to admit I made a mistake." Likewise Lydon made it clear that PiL as a collaborative corporation was no more:
1978: "In this band we are all equal. No Rod Stewarts."
1986: "PiL is technically me, officially me, and anybody I work with on my songs. They are my songs."

'Album' featured seven tracks, three co-written by Lydon with Laswell ('Home', 'Rise' and 'FFF'), the remainder with Bruni and/or Schulz. Of the three Lydon/Laswell songs only 'Rise' was a progression, though 'Home' was a most respectable reproduction of the 'First Issue' sound. 'FFF' shares more in common with the other four compositions, being virtually an exercise in heavy metal, something Lydon was mightily amused to see upset old fans.

Ironically when 'Album' did appear the critical response was generally enthusiastic. The *Sounds* reviewer gave the album five stars and opined, "The best metal album I've ever heard"; while Gavin Martin's review in *NME* had the headline 'Good' in case you weren't sure what he thought of it after reading the review. Even *Smash Hits* considered the album, "Gross, lazy and occasionally magnificent."

Melody Maker was the only dissenting voice, and thankfully they were brutally negative about the album. The Legendary Stud Brothers considered it, "complacent, sluggish and apathetic" and concluded, "This 'Album' is not dangerous, it's not subversive, it's not new, it's not Public Image Ltd."

As if to prove the point that 'Rise' did not represent 'Album', and perhaps learning his lesson from the failure of 'Bad Life', Lydon released a follow-up single in April 1986, three months after 'Rise' and two months after 'Album'. 'Home' and its B-side 'Round' – both lifted from the album – proved PiL's worst selling single to date, reaching only 75 in the charts for a single week.

The failure of the single did not help plans, already afoot, for a May tour of the UK. Lydon had once again decided to form a new version of PiL to play live, but the bad press the previous tour received and the failure of 'Home' did not make a 1986 tour as attractive a commercial proposition as the 1983 tour, when many fans turned up more out of a sense of idle curiosity than galvanised by the crashing brilliance of 'Live In Tokyo'.

CHAPTER 12

'The worst lie is that I make music only as an elaborate joke'

"The worst lie is that I make music only as an elaborate joke." John Lydon, May 1986

If Lydon wanted his music to be treated seriously, then opening PiL's May 1986 shows with an instrumental version of Led Zeppelin's 'Kashmir' hardly seemed the way to go about it. What it did provide was a salutary pointer to the content of the remainder of the show: a hotch-potch of songs from assorted PiL epochs, played in much the same manner throughout, with an over-emphasis on a style of playing which stripped the early songs of their jagged edges and made the latter songs smoothly indistinctive. And once again there was a solitary Pistols song, devoid of its original spark. This time it was 'Pretty Vacant'.

Lydon's decision not to tour with any musicians from the live band he played with in the States required him to put a band together quickly. Yet when the UK tour was announced at the beginning of April – an extensive bout of dates, 16 in all, climaxing with a gig at Brixton's Academy on May 27 – he was also able to announce the band which featured the relatively unknown Alan Dais on bass, Bruce Smith on drums, Lu Edmons on keyboards and the some-what better known John McGeoch on guitar.

McGeoch is to date Lydon's most recent collaborator, the last of a string of guitarists with varying musical and creative pedigrees who have worked – inevitably for a short period – with him. McGeoch's name was certainly a salvaging factor when the tour was announced. He had spent considerable time as a member of Magazine and Siouxsie And The Banshees, two of the premier bands in the vanguard of New Wave acts who succeeded the punk revolution (along with the likes of PiL and Joy Division).

According to McGeoch, he was originally asked by Keith Bourton, who had now replaced Larry White as Lydon's manager, and a meeting was duly arranged, "John had just come over from America. We had met before and spent some time together in New York in 1982. We introduced ourselves and we got on well, so he popped the question and there wasn't much of a decision to

be made. I said, 'Oh definitely, let's do it'."

McGeoch's guitar style had some similarities to Levene's, which would hopefully mean a return to the more distinctive metallic sound that had previously been a PiL trademark. McGeoch's presence at least suggested the 1986 tour was a more serious endeavour than the cabaret tour in the autumn of 1983.

But McGeoch's contribution, though undoubtedly an improvement on the 1983 incarnation, was a profound disappointment. His guitar-sound failed to dominate the music and the disappointment for some in the audience was so profound that Lydon found himself in physical danger on-stage for the first time since the Ritz gig.

On the first night of the tour, at Hanley Victoria Hall ... "A bottle hit Dear John on the head, halfway through the first song," according to the *NME* reviewer who seemed unsympathetic, informing Lydon that contempt can work two ways: "Showing contempt for one's audience is nothing new where John's concerned, but when they bite back it's not so much fun."

The following night at Sheffield City Hall the missile was more dangerous – a billiard ball, though thankfully it missed its target. Sensibly, Lydon called a halt to the proceedings. In Sheffield Lydon also ran into one journalist who actually recalled the early PiL, Mick Middles (who had reviewed the February '79 'Creation For Liberation' gig for *Sounds*), and who was pre-pared to give Lydon a hard time about his current stance:

Q: "Tonight you'll be playing Sex Pistols songs. Isn't that playing to the whims of the people who still come to see Johnny Rotten?"
A: "It's pampering to no one's whims but mine."
Q: "But you're verging on self-parody."
A: "No, not at all. You just get me, wonderful me, and nothing else."

Lydon refused to deal with the theme of Middles' enquiry, the abandonment of the PiL ideals, insisting ... "What goes on on the PiL stage is entirely my concern. Mine and nobody else. If I want to play 'Anarchy In The UK' all night I

Lydon and McGeoch.

will do. What right have you to tell me what to play?" Middles was unconvinced and closed his article in *Muze* with the epitaph, "Johnny Rotten is dead. Long live the parody."

The poor reviews, combined with bad memories of the 1983 tour, had a discernible effect on the attendance at many gigs, most of which were less than full. This was hardly surprising considering the venom of most of the reviews. "You come from a time when you were slagged for being brilliant, today you're getting kicked for having a set full of shit." So wrote the *Sounds* reviewer who attended the Scarborough show.

The tour wound to an unsatisfactory close when trouble at the solitary London show forced the band to cut their set short (omitting 'Time Zone' and 'Ease'). General dissatisfaction about the whole performance from assorted Brixton attendees sparked a battle between punters and bouncers which apparently, "almost toppled over the PA stacks". When the band continued touring in the States in June and July matters had not improved. The *LA Times* reviewer of PiL's Hollywood Palladium show observed: "It was some fireworks aimed at the stage – along with spit, beer and other 1976-era punk missiles – that

Clockwise from left: Lou Edmonds, Bruce Smith, Allan Dias, Johnny Lydon and John McGeoch.

brought PiL's performance to a premature halt early on."

For some reason the truly appalling 1983 line-up had escaped unscathed from their European shows, despite the understandable desire among some fans to do to them what they were doing to PiL's music. Yet the far more satisfactory Lydon/McGeoch line-up ended up in physical danger. The constant threat of serious harm inflicted on a member of PiL was finally realised in September 1986, on a tour of Europe. At the Vienna show on September 12, McGeoch was hit in the face by a two-litre wine bottle and had to have 40 stitches in his face. The remainder of the tour was promptly cancelled.

However despite a subsequent statement from the PiL office that, "the new PiL line-up's whole touring future is now in jeopardy", the band returned for a further European tour a year later, to somewhat similar treatment. At an Italian show, Robin Gibson of *Sounds* observed, "Tonight they intend to scale 'Four Enclosed Walls' from 'Flowers Of Romance'. But the set is cut short due to a small rock-throwing element, being decidedly too 'honest about how they feel'."

McGeoch had stated, during the May 1986 tour, that the new PiL line-up would be recording a new album after the European tour. However the follow-up to 'Album' was not forthcoming and it would be 18 months after the release of 'Album', and a year after the Vienna incident, before sight or sound would be heard of PiL again.

In fact PiL had been in America, playing a few shows and writing new material, though recording would take place in England. For the first time since 'Flowers Of Romance' the material was collectively credited to the whole band. On August 10, 1987 the first studio recordings of this PiL line-up were released. The single was called 'Seattle' and its flip-side was appropriately entitled 'Selfish Rubbish'.

Also included on the 12-inch was a new version of 'The Suit'. Apparently during days off from recording the new PiL album, entitled 'Happy?', Lydon and McGeoch had re-recorded new arrangements of some old PiL songs for a

budget album to be called 'Renovations'. The album was in fact never issued, though a further song from the project, 'Religion', was included on the 12-inch version of 'The Body', the follow-up single to 'Seattle'.

Surprisingly, given the fact that generally PiL singles issued to promote an imminent album had previously gone Top 10, 'Seattle' barely cracked the Top 30. The riff was probably too meandering to gain enough airplay, and PiL's epoch as a 'singles band' had been falsely sustained beyond the band's truly creative era by a couple of classic singles in the form of 'This Is Not A Love Song' and 'Rise'. 'Seattle' was no classic, albeit still a notch above most chart material in 1987.

However there was a discernible lack of interest this time around in The Return (again) Of Johnny Rotten. A tour scheduled for September 1987, to promote the September 14 release of 'Happy?', was cut to only five dates when bassist Alan Dais sprained his wrist and was unable to play the scheduled shows in early September. In fact the shows were not selling well anyway and the five remaining gigs were primarily in PiL 'strongholds': Edinburgh, Manchester and two gigs in London (where Lydon was always assured an audience, albeit not always an appreciative one).

The album 'Happy?' showed little development on the sound of 'Album', though when Lydon was informed of this he told journalist Robin Gibson he had cloth-ears. In the *Sounds* review Ron Rom gave the album four stars, but wrote, "You wouldn't mention 'Happy?' in the same breath as 'Second Edition' or 'Flowers Of Romance'."

Of course Lydon was delighted with the album, as he usually was with any product which had just come off the conveyor-belt, proclaiming it to be . . . "A magnificent piece of work . . . a diamond in a mud-pack of mediocrity." The saddest thing about the album was the sheer lack of controversy it generated. Rather the album met with apathy in the UK, as indeed did the five shows at the end of the month. This time around the statutory Pistols song was 'Holidays In The Sun', as Lydon continued slowly disembowelling most of the 'Never

Mind The Bollocks' album. In the interim the cancelled gigs remained unscheduled, and will presumably stay that way until Lydon and his band have further product to ply.

At the conclusion of a February 1986 interview Lydon commented: "You do realise that in a year's time I will have contradicted everything I've said just now." For once he was very close to the truth. Unfortunately Lydon has as a result used up any remaining credibility long ago. It was bad enough that he did not deliver what he promised with his brave new experiment – Public Image Limited. Far worse, however, was that he gave up trying.

"This is what you want/ This is what you get."

Ironically, if Lydon had issued 'Album' and 'Happy' straight after his departure from The Pistols, they would probably have been well received by public and press alike. Throughout PiL's career many a journalist has suspected that Lydon was having one massive joke at their expense. Yet it was only after the supreme parody – the 1983 tour – that certain members of the press were finally convinced that the original PiL was not an elaborate joke, though only because they could now see what real parody was all about.

Since 1981 Lydon has enjoyed the advantage that comes with time blurring the edges of memory. Simply by continually using the PiL name after Levene's departure, PiL have become synonymous with something entirely different from what they originally stood for. Today the 'group' is only dimly concerned with what came before – directly influenced but only through refracted glass. PiL have become 'PiL'.

In reality PiL was a failed experiment. Wobble was right when he said they would not win. However it was an audacious attempt to avoid the pitfalls of conventional music industry wisdom. At least the band was aware of the need for something profoundly different from punk and brave enough to pursue it. That the experiment failed does not invalidate the experiment.

In their five-year career PiL issued three of the finest albums of the last decade: 'First Issue', 'Metal Box' and 'Commercial Zone'. The début

Johnny Rotten and wife Nora at a London party to launch new Smith/Jones
book and record, 'Monday'.

album is now appreciated for the seminal record it was, and 'Metal Box' remains a signpost on the edge of modern music, even if 'Commercial Zone' is still not well enough known or appreciated. It is this heritage which Lydon has misused since 1983. The live versions of songs from the first four PiL albums are not merely inferior these days but – stripped of their context – are devoid of the power they once held.

If PiL's ideas about extending their interests beyond what they saw as the parochial niche they carved out in modern music came to naught – no matter. If the band never completed a film soundtrack, maybe it was because no movies were being made which could accommodate their sound. If the band's visual conceptions came to nothing, it was because they had a genuine desire to break out of the three-minute-promo-video syndrome and had neither the finance nor the expertise to do it. If the talk of videos and film soundtracks hinted of some grand scheme on the band's part, it kept the media guessing about how serious such endeavours were. Ironically PiL were ahead of their time in one way at least – they were the ultimate CD band. If CD was invented for any particular band it was PiL, whose studio recordings cried out for true hi-fidelity reproduction.

Of course the focal point of the band – especially live – was always Lydon, but PiL was formed as a co-operative venture and could never be anything but a co-operative. What would be commendable ideals when motivated by a collective design would come across as pure arrogance when expounded by one individual.

Ultimately I fail to understand why Lydon should not have simply dissolved PiL in 1983 and formed The John Lydon Band. As such, if he so wished, he could still play material from all his past recordings. However though he tried to escape The Pistols' myth, he in turn imbued PiL with its own mystique, and this time he did not discard the mystique but rather used it to try and build a new career. Instead he chose to dismantle that mystique brick by brick with each new 'PiL' product.

In the history of modern music there are numerous examples of bands continuing under their original name, even when the initial creative spark supplied by certain individuals within the band has long since departed. Fairport Convention, Fleetwood Mac, Pink Floyd, The Doors and The Clash all spring to mind, not to mention numerous black vocal groups from the sixties. Occasionally the new incarnations produce material of worth, but such worth remains tarnished by its counterfeit image. Rather than standing on its own, the new material is inevitably compared with the previous incarnation's finest hour, against which it can never stand up. That is Lydon's problem, and it is one of his own making – that whatever he may issue under the PiL logo must stand up against 'Metal Box' not 'Album'.

In 1972 a band calling itself The Velvet Underground toured the UK. Led by Doug Yule, they had no connection with what The Velvet Underground ever stood for. It was Doug Yule's band. But no one would pay to see the Doug Yule band. It featured neither Lou Reed nor John Cale. In 1987 a band calling itself Public Image Limited toured the UK. It featured neither Keith Levene nor Jah Wobble – and while Lydon sits at the side of the stage, maybe thinking about those remarkable 1980 shows, the parody dances.

"The public image belongs to me. It's my entrance, my own creation . . . "

1978

JANUARY 14 The Sex Pistols play their last gig at The Winterland in San Francisco. Johnny Rotten's last comment before leaving the stage becomes the band's epitaph, "Ever get the feeling you've been cheated."

JANUARY TO FEBRUARY Rotten 'crashes' at photographer Joe Stevens' apartment in New York for a couple of weeks in the wake of The Pistols' demise.

MARCH 4 *Sounds* publishes the first part of a two-part interview with John Lydon in Jamaica, conducted by Vivien Goldman who had travelled to Jamaica with him.

MAY 27 First press article on Lydon's new band in *New Musical Express*. The line-up consists of John Lydon (vocals), Jah Wobble (bass), Jim Walker (drums) and Keith Levene (guitar).

JULY 22 Caroline Coon interviews Lydon's as yet unnamed band for *Sounds*. The title of the article is taken from one of the songs she hears the band perform, 'Public Image'.

JULY TO NOVEMBER PiL work on their first album at various studios including The Manor in Oxfordshire and Shepherd's Bush Studios, Advision Studios and Wessex Studios in London.

SEPTEMBER 1978 The release of Jah Wobble's first solo single, 'Dreadlock Don't Deal With Wedlock'/'Pthilius Pubis' (VOLE 9). Adverts for the single urge fans to, "Snap it up before we reprocess the vinyl."

SEPTEMBER 15 The recording of the video for 'Public Image'. This is subsequently released on 'Videos' (VVC 144).

OCTOBER 13 The release of 'Public Image'/'Cowboy Song' (VS 228).

OCTOBER 14 Adverts appear for the 'Public Image' single – produced by 'Public Image Ltd': "A product of your society."

OCTOBER The video of 'Public Image' is broadcast on *Saturday Night People*.

OCTOBER 21 'Public Image' enters the chart, peaking at number nine and remaining in the charts eight weeks.

OCTOBER 28 Lydon is interviewed on Radio One's *Rock On* programme.

DECEMBER 8 Release of 'Public Image – First Issue' (V 2114). Tracks: Theme/Religion I/Religion II/Annalisa/Public Image/Low Life/ Attack/Fodderstompf.

DECEMBER 9 Adverts appear for 'First Issue' with a Hollywood-style photograph of Lydon and the announcement: 'Public Image – An album is born'.

MID-DECEMBER BRUSSELS. PiL's first live gig. The set lasts only six songs.

MID-DECEMBER PARIS: Theme, Low Life, Annalisa, Religion, Public Image, Belsen Was A Gas, Attack, Problems, Public Image II,

Annalisa II. The first seven songs are included on a bootleg called 'Recorded In Paris When Nobody Was Looking'.

DECEMBER 23 'First Issue' enters the album charts, peaking at 22 and remaining in the charts for 11 weeks.

DECEMBER 25 RAINBOW THEATRE, LONDON.

DECEMBER 26 RAINBOW THEATRE, LONDON: Theme, Low Life, Belsen Was A Gas, Annalisa, Public Image, Religion, Attack, Public Image II. The gig is bootlegged on an album called 'Extra Issue'. The bootleg is subsequently re-pressed as 'Nubes'.

DECEMBER 1978 TO JANUARY 1979 According to the band they re-recorded the first album for Warner Brothers in the States. These sessions took place prior to commencing recording the second album and presumably featured Walker on drums. This version of the album was never issued. Probably recorded at around the same time, if not at the same sessions, was the original version of 'Home Is Where The Heart Is', a song for which Walker shares composing credits but which was not issued until 1981.

1979

JANUARY The release of 'Steel Leg Vs. The Electric Dread', a 12-inch EP (VS 23912) featuring Jah Wobble and Keith Levene (as 'Stratetime Keith'). The tracks are: Steel Leg/Stratetime And The Wide Man/Haile Unlikely By The Electric Dread/ Unlikely Pub.

JANUARY Drummer Jim Walker quits PiL.

JANUARY TO FEBRUARY PiL search for a replacement drummer for Jim Walker. Vivien Jackson, who has worked with Linton Kwesi Johnson, is the first replacement; but is in turn quickly replaced by Dave Humphries (who is the drummer on the Manchester show).

JANUARY 20 In the *NME* Readers Poll for 1978 PiL are voted 'Best New Group' and 'Second Best Single' and Lydon is voted 'Best Singer'.

FEBRUARY 14 Mr Justice Browne-Wilkinson rules that a receiver be appointed to safeguard the assets of Glitterbest, The Sex Pistols' management company. Lydon has won the first round in his battle to wrestle control of The Pistols' name and monies from McLaren.

FEBRUARY 16 – PiL are scheduled to play the Dublin Arts Project Centre but the gig is cancelled when the band fail to find a drummer in time.

FEBRUARY 23 'CREATION FOR LIBERATION' CONCERT, KING'S HALL, BELLE VUE, MANCHESTER: Theme, Annalisa, Low Life, Religion, Attack, Belsen Was A Gas, Public Image, Annalisa II.

FEBRUARY 24 In *Sounds* Readers Poll for 1978 PiL are voted 'Second Best New Group', 'Best Single' and Lydon is voted 'Second Best Singer'.

MARCH Probable date for the start of sessions for recording PiL's second album. Certainly recorded at this time is 'Death Disco' which does not feature Jim Walker or Richard Dudanski on drums. Possibly Dave Humphries or Levene played drums on the track.

APRIL Richard Dudanski is recruited as the new PiL drummer. He had previously worked with the 101'ers and The Raincoats.

APRIL TO AUGUST The bulk of what is to become 'Metal Box' is completed at sessions with Richard Dudanski on drums. Songs certainly recorded at this time include 'Albatross', 'Memories', 'Another' (an instrumental version of which appears on the album, entitled 'Graveyard'), 'And No Birds Do Sing', 'Chant' and 'Socialist'.

MAY 31 John Lydon appears on *Juke Box Jury* on BBC1.

JUNE 18 RUSSELL'S CLUB, MANCHESTER: Chant, Death Disco, Memories, Public Image I, Public Image II, Public Image III, Annalisa, And No Birds Do Sing, Albatross.

JUNE 29 The release of 'Death Disco'/'And No Birds Do Sing' (VS 274) seven-inch single; and 'Death Disco' (½ Mix)/Megamix ('Fodderstompf') (VS 27412) 12-inch single. The 12-inch version of 'Death Disco' is some six minutes longer than the seven-inch version. 'Megamix' is an instrumental version of 'Fodderstompf'. Released at the same time is Jah Wobble's own single 'Dan McArthur' (aka 'Disco Dummy')/'Dan McArthur II' (VS 275).

JULY 2 PiL make their first live appearance on TV, on Tyne Tees' *Check It Out* on which they perform 'Chant'. Afterwards the band are supposed to be interviewed, but when Lydon is provoked he storms off the set, shortly followed by Wobble, Levene and Dudanski.

JULY 7 'Death Disco' enters the charts, peaking at number 20 and remaining in the charts for seven weeks.

JULY 9 The recording of the video for 'Death Disco'. This is subsequently included on 'Videos' (VVC 144).

JULY PiL appear live on *Top Of The Pops* performing 'Death Disco'.

JULY 26 John Lydon is interviewed by Robin Valk for Birmingham's radio station, BRMB.

AUGUST 10 John Lydon and Keith Levene are interviewed for Radio Merseyside.

SEPTEMBER 8 LEEDS SCI-FI FESTIVAL, QUEENS HALL, LEEDS: Chant, Annalisa, Memories, Low Life, Public Image, Attack, Death Disco, Another, And No Birds Do Sing. The entire gig is bootlegged on an album, 'Sci-Fi'.

SEPTEMBER Dudanski quits PiL after the Leeds Sci-Fi gig. His initial replacement is apparently Karl Burns of The Fall, but his tenure is only very brief. Martin Atkins is then auditioned for the position. His audition apparently consisted of the studio recording of 'Bad Baby' subsequently included on 'Metal Box'.

SEPTEMBER TO OCTOBER The final sessions for 'Metal Box', probably with Levene (or maybe Atkins) on drums. Songs which are products of the last few sessions include 'Poptones', 'Careering', 'The Suit' and 'Radio Four'.

OCTOBER 10 The release of 'Memories'/'Another' as both seven-inch (VS 299) and 12-inch (VS 29912).

October 20 'Memories' enters the charts, peaking at number 60 and remaining in the charts for two weeks.

NOVEMBER Lydon and Levene are interviewed on Radio One's *Rock On* by Trevor Dan, to publicise the release of 'Metal Box'.

NOVEMBER 23 The release of 'Metal Box' (METAL 1) an album consisting of three 12-inch records playing at 45 rpm. The tracks are: I: Albatross/ Memories/Swan Lake. II: Poptones/Careering/No Birds/ Graveyard. III: The Suit/Bad Baby/Socialist/Chant/Radio Four. The insert with the album lists two private members of Public Image Limited – Dave Crowe and Jeanette Lee.

NOVEMBER 24 The highly enthusiastic review of 'Metal Box' in *New Musical Express* warrants a front-cover for PiL. The advert for the album which appears in this week's *NME* consists of the lyrics to the album (uncredited) with just 'Public Image Limited' at the top of the page and 'The Metal Box' at the bottom.

DECEMBER 8 'Metal Box' enters the charts, peaking at number 18 and remaining in the charts for eight weeks.

DECEMBER 17 – The broadcast of a session for John Peel's show by the band. Recorded at the BBC Maida Vale Studios in London the songs represent Martin Atkins' formal début with PiL. The three songs broadcast are 'Chant', 'Poptones' and 'Careering'.

1980

JANUARY 17 THE PALACE, PARIS: Careering, Poptones, Annalisa, Death Disco, Memories, Public Image, Chant, Low Life, Attack, And No Birds Do Sing, Another, Bad Baby. 'Careering', 'Chant', 'Poptones' and 'Attack' from tonight's show are later included on 'Paris Au Printemps' (V 2183).

JANUARY 18 THE PALACE, PARIS: Chant, Careering, Annalisa, Low Life, Bad Baby, Public Image, Theme. 'Low Life', 'Bad Baby' and 'Theme' from tonight's show are later included on 'Paris Au Printemps' (V 2183).

FEBRUARY 5 PiL appear on BBC2's *The Old Grey Whistle Test* on which they perform 'Poptones' and 'Careering'. Both tracks subsequently appear on the triple bootleg set, 'Force'.

FEBRUARY 22 The release of 'Second Edition' (VD 2512), a conventional double-album version of 'Metal Box'. The order of the tracks is slightly changed to fit the four-side format. It now runs: Albatross/Memories/Swan Lake/Poptones/Careering/Socialist/ Graveyard/The Suit/Bad Baby/No Birds/Chant/Radio Four. Unfortunately when the CD version (CDVD 2512) is released it is this order which is utilised.

MARCH Lydon and Levene fly to the West Coast to conduct a series of interviews with the likes of *Rolling Stone*, the *L.A. Times* and the *San Francisco Chronicle* and to appear at a press conference arranged by PiL's American label Warner Bros at The City, San Francisco.

MARCH 8 'Second Edition' enters the charts, peaking at 46 and remaining in the charts for two weeks.

APRIL 16 PiL are interviewed on the WBCN-FM radio station.

APRIL 17 PiL are interviewed on the WERS-FM radio station.

APRIL 18 THE ORPHEUM, BOSTON: Careering, Annalisa, Attack, Poptones, Low Life, Public Image, Fodderstompf, Death Disco, Bad Baby, Home Is Where The Heart Is, Theme, Chant, Another, Instrumental, Public Image, Memories, Poptones.

APRIL 20 NEW YORK PALLADIUM: Bad Baby (instrumental), Careering, Annalisa, Attack, Low Life, Fodderstompf, Death Disco, Memories, Public Image, Another, Poptones, Bad Baby, Instrumental. A member of the audience films about 10 minutes of 8mm footage during this show.

APRIL CHICAGO, ILLINOIS.

APRIL THE AGORA, ATLANTA: Bad Baby (instrumental), Careering, Chant, Annalisa, Poptones, Attack, Low Life, Public Image, Death Disco, Memories, Careering.

APRIL 26 THE TOWER, PHILADELPHIA: Careering, Annalisa, Poptones, Low Life, Attack, Chant, Memories, Public Image, Death Disco, Bad Baby.

APRIL 28 MOTOR CITY ROLLER-RINK, DETROIT: Careering, Annalisa, Attack, Low Life, Chant, Poptones, My Generation/Public Image, Death Disco, Memories.

MAY 1 Lydon and Levene's March interview with Mikal Gilmore is published in *Rolling Stone*, far and away the most important American music paper.

MAY 3 PiL 'perform' on NBC's *American Bandstand*. Lydon mimes to 'Poptones' and 'Careering'.

MAY 4 OLYMPIC AUDITORIUM, LOS ANGELES: Fodderstompf, Careering, Annalisa, Attack, Low Life, Chant, Death Disco, Poptones, Religion, Bad Baby, Public Image, Memories, Home Is Where The Heart Is. This gig (minus 'Memories', which is however credited on the sleeve) is bootlegged as a double-album called 'Profile'. The album is later reviewed in *Melody Maker*. A member of the audience also films about 10 minutes of 8mm footage during this show.

MAY 6 OAKLAND AUDITORIUM.

MAY 8 Jah Wobble's solo album, 'The Legend Lives On' (V 2158), is released. The tracks are: Betrayal/Beat The Drum/ Blueberry Hill/ Not Another/ Tales From Outer Space/ Today Is The First Day Of The Rest Of My Life/ Dan McArthur/ Pineapple.

MAY A single is issued from Jah Wobble's solo album: 'Betrayal'/ 'Battle Of Britain By Mr X' (VS 33712).

MAY 10 PiL are interviewed on KTIM radio in the afternoon. SOUTH Of MARKET CULTURAL CENTRE, SAN FRANCISCO: Bad Baby, Careering, Annalisa, Attack, Low Life, Chant, Death Disco, Public Image, Poptones, Home Is Where The Heart Is, Memories.

JUNE Jah Wobble issues further material from 'The Legend Lives On' sessions on a 12-inch mini-album entitled 'V.S.EP Featuring Blueberry Hill' (VS 36112). Though assigned a 12-inch single

catalogue number the record plays at 33⅓ pm and clocks in at 34 minutes. The tracks are Blueberry Hill/Blueberry Hill (Computer Version)/I Need You By My Side/A Message From Pluto/Seaside Special/Something Profound/Blood Repression.

JUNE 27 Lydon and Levene appear on Tom Snyder's prime time American TV programme, *The Tomorrow Show*. Their appearance, and the barely disguised mutual hostility between the participants, generates substantial controversy in the US.

JUNE 28 It is announced in the UK music press that Martin Atkins has left PiL.

JULY The departure of original bassist, Jah Wobble, who has become dissatisfied with Lydon and Levene's attitude towards their audience. Around this time Dave Crowe also leaves the organisation.

OCTOBER 3 Lydon is involved in a fracas with the landlord of a pub in Dublin's Eden Quay. He is subsequently arrested for assault, despite being the only individual to be injured in the incident.

OCTOBER 6 Lydon is sentenced to three months in prison by a Dublin court. He is released on bail pending an appeal.

OCTOBER Virgin Records issue a various artists compilation called 'Machines' (V 2177). It includes a previously unreleased PiL instrumental, probably from the 'Metal Box' sessions, called 'Pied Piper'.

LATE OCTOBER TO EARLY NOVEMBER Lydon and Levene re-recruit Martin Atkins on a day-to-day basis to help them commence work on PiL's third studio album at The Manor Studios in Oxfordshire. Sessions last approximately 10 days and appear to have resulted in four songs for the 'Flowers Of Romance' album: 'Four Enclosed Walls', 'Under The House', 'Banging The Door' and 'Hymnie's Him'; plus a re-dubbed version of 'Home Is Where The Heart Is'.

NOVEMBER 14 The release of 'Paris Au Printemps' (V 2183), a live album drawn from PiL's two shows in January. The tracks are: Theme/Chant/Careering/Bad Baby/Lowlife/Attack/Poptones.

NOVEMBER Lydon and Levene, with Jeanette Lee providing her own suggestions but no musical input, continue work on the 'Flowers Of Romance' album at Townhouse Studios in London. The remainder of the album is completed in a second 10-day stint of sessions.

NOVEMBER 22 'Paris Au Printemps' enters the charts, peaking at 61 and remaining in the charts for two weeks.

DECEMBER Lydon and Levene are interviewed on Radio One's *Rock On* programme, promoting the 'Paris Au Printemps' album. They also premier the title-track of the now-completed 'Flowers Of Romance' album, though it has not yet received its final mix.

1981

MARCH 27 The release of 'Flowers Of Romance'/'Home Is Where The Heart Is' (VS 397) seven-inch single and 'Flowers Of Romance'/ 'Flowers Of Romance' (instrumental)/'Home Is Where The Heart Is' (VS 39712) 12-inch single.

APRIL 4 'Flowers Of Romance' enters the single charts, peaking at number 24 and remaining in the charts for seven weeks.

APRIL Lydon, Levene and Lee appear on *Top Of The Pops* miming to a version of 'Flowers Of Romance'.

APRIL 10 The release of the 'Flowers Of Romance' album (V 2189). Tracks are: Four Enclosed Walls/Track 8/Phenagen/Flowers Of Romance/Under The House/Hymie's Him/Banging The Door/Go Back/Francis Massacre.

APRIL 18 'Flowers Of Romance' enters the album charts, peaking at number 11 and remaining in the charts for five weeks.

MAY 15 THE RITZ, NEW YORK: Flowers Of Romance, Four Enclosed Walls, Go Back. For this show PiL recruit a drummer, Sam Ulano. However he is little utilised and is not recruited on a permanent basis. A bootleg EP of the full performance is later issued, entitled 'The Famous Riot Show'.

MAY 19 PiL conduct a press conference at Warner Brothers Records' conference room in New York.

AUGUST The release of a single by Vivien Goldman called 'Laundrette'/'Private Armies' (WIN 1). The single is co-produced by Goldman, Levene and Lydon; Levene also providing guitar and bass whilst Lydon "provided cash and atmosphere."

1982

JANUARY 29 A report in *Sounds* suggests that PiL have 'disintegrated'.

FEBRUARY 6 PiL deny that they have split up in the *New Musical Express*. Also revealed is that the band have a new member, Ken Lockie (on keyboards).

SPRING Keith Levene runs into Martin Atkins at New York's Mudd Club. Atkins is performing with his band Brian Brain. Atkins is invited to work on the fourth PiL album, which they are due to start recording.

SPRING TO SUMMER Levene and Lydon, along with Atkins, finally enter South Park recording studios in New York to commence work on the follow-up to 'Flowers Of Romance'. Songs probably recorded in initial sessions include 'Blue Water', 'Where Are You (Lou Reed Part Two)', 'Lou Reed Part One', 'The Slab (Order Of Death)', 'Miller High Life' and 'Mad Max (Bad Life)'.

MAY TO JULY John Lydon works on a new film, tentatively entitled *Psycho Jogger*, starring with Harvey Keitel. Initial filming takes place in New York and is followed by six weeks filming in Rome. All the while Levene is ensconced in the studio working on songs.

AUGUST 7 *NMF* editor Neil Spencer interviews John Lydon whilst Lydon is in London for a few days late in July en route from Rome to New York. It is published in *New Musical Express* on this date. In the interview Lydon insists that PiL is back as a working unit. Jeanette Lee, who has travelled with Lydon to Rome and then London, ceases to be a member of PiL, deciding to remain in London rather than return to New York with Lydon.

SUMMER Pete Jones, bassist in Brian Brain, is recruited into PiL, enabling the band to resume live performances.

SEPTEMBER 28 ROSELAND BALLROOM, NEW YORK: Where Are You, Public Image, Death Disco, Annalisa, Attack, Religion, Under The House, Chant, Public Image.

OCTOBER 7 THE CHANNEL, BOSTON.

OCTOBER 15 MONTREAL.

OCTOBER 16 CONCERT HALL, TORONTO: Lou Reed Part One, Where Are You, Annalisa, Bad Baby, Public Image, Religion, Death Disco, Mad Max, Attack, Chant, Under The House.

OCTOBER 23 GRANADA THEATRE, CHICAGO.

OCTOBER 25 FIRST AVENUE THEATRE, MINNEAPOLIS: Where Are You, Annalisa, Bad Baby, Careering, Religion, Attack, Chant, Mad Max.

EARLY NOVEMBER PiL hold a press conference at Le Dome in Hollywood. They announce the formation of a new label to distribute their records, Public Enterprise Productions; and a new 'communications' company, Multi Image Corporation, to handle other PiL activities. They also announce the imminent release of a new album, 'You Are Now Entering A Commercial Zone' and a new single 'Blue Water'.

NOVEMBER 5 GALLERIA, SAN FRANCISCO. At the soundcheck PiL perform: Public Image (instrumental), Where Are You, Mad Max, Annalisa, Hymnie's Him, And No Birds Do Sing. At the gig they play: Blue Water, Where Are You, Annalisa, Bad Baby, Attack, Chant, Careering, Religion, Mad Max, Public Image, Death Disco, Low Life, And No Birds Do Sing, Public Image, Under The House.

NOVEMBER 7 PASADENA CONVENTION CENTRE: Lou Reed Part One, Where Are You, Annalisa, Religion, Bad Baby, Attack, Careering, Mad Max, Chant, Death Disco, Low Life, Public Image, Under The House. The whole gig is featured on a triple bootleg 'album' (actually three 12-inch singles) entitled 'Force'.

NOVEMBER 8 PASADENA CONVENTION CENTRE: A second show was added at the last minute and poorly attended. According to *Hot Wacks XII* there is a single bootleg album from this gig called simply 'Live In Pasadena' and featuring nine tracks: Theme, Where Are You, Religion, Careering, Death Disco, Mad Max, Low Life, Public Image, Under The House.

NOVEMBER 10 ELITE CLUB, CALIFORNIA: Blue Water, Theme, Where Are You, Annalisa, Death Disco, And No Birds Do Sing,

Careering, Mad Max, Attack, Religion, Bad Baby, Chant, Low Life, Public Image.

NOVEMBER 13 SHRINE AUDITORIUM, LOS ANGELES.

NOVEMBER 21 Keith Levene marries his long-standing girlfriend, Lori.

DECEMBER 11 ATLANTA, GEORGIA: Blue Water, Theme, Where Are You, Annalisa, Bad Baby, Religion, Careering, Chant, And No Birds Do Sing, Mad Max, Death Disco, Public Image, Attack, Under The House.

DECEMBER 31 CLUB NETWORK, LONG BEACH.

1983

JANUARY 29 BROOKLYN ZOO, NEW YORK: Public Image, Blue Water, Where Are You, Annalisa, Bad Baby, Careering, Religion, Mad Max, Theme, Death Disco, Chant, Attack.

JANUARY 29 PiL are filmed for Italian TV, at the Brooklyn Zoo in New York, performing 'Religion' and 'Chant'. The footage is probably from a soundcheck and presumably dates from the day of PiL's January gig.

MARCH The world première in Rome of the film starring John Lydon and Harvey Keitel, now entitled *Order Of Death*.

MARCH 26 PARAMOUNT THEATRE, STATEN ISLAND, NEW YORK: Where Are You, Mad Max, Under The House, Banging The Door, Chant, Careering, Bad Baby, Death Disco, Annalisa. The gig is issued as a bootleg album called 'Where Are We'.

MARCH 30 POUGHKEEPSIE, NEW YORK STATE: Where Are You, Annalisa, Bad Baby, Religion, Low Life, Careering, Chant, Death Disco, Public Image, Under The House.

MAY 14 It is announced in the UK press that Pete Jones, the bassist, has left PiL.

JUNE 4 It is announced in the UK music press that Keith Levene has quit PiL, having become "increasingly at odds, musically and corporately, with the others."

JUNE Lydon recruits a band of PiL clones called Westside Frankie and The Inglewood Jerks to replace Jones and Levene. Atkins remains in the band. The new musicians are Joseph Guda (guitar), Louie Bernardi (bass) and Tom Zvoncheck (keyboards).

JUNE 10 The new 'PiL' play the Hollywood Palladium in Los Angeles. They encore with 'Anarchy In The UK'.

JUNE 21 NAKANO SUN PLAZA, TOKYO. 'PiL' commence their first Japanese tour.

JUNE 24 NAGOYA CITY HALL.

JUNE 25 OSAKA WELFARE INSURANCE HALL.

JUNE 27 NAKANO SUN PLAZA, TOKYO.

JUNE 28 NAKANO SUN PLAZA, TOKYO.

JULY 1 NAKANO SUN PLAZA, TOKYO. This show is filmed and is later released as a Virgin official video, 'PiL Live'. The songs featured on the video are: Low Life, Annalisa, Religion, Flowers Of Romance, Death Disco, This Is Not A Love Song, Public Image. This is also one of two shows recorded digitally for a live album, creatively entitled 'Live In Tokyo'.

JULY 2 NAKANO SUN PLAZA, TOKYO. The second show to be recorded for the Japanese live album, 'Live In Tokyo'.

JULY 5 NAKANO SUN PLAZA, TOKYO.

SEPTEMBER 5 The release of 'This Is Not A Love Song'/'Public Image' (VS 529) 7-inch single; and 'This Is Not A Love Song'/'Blue Water'/'This Is Not A Love Song' (remix)/'Public Image' (VS 52912) 12-inch single.

SEPTEMBER 12 The recording of the video for 'This Is Not A Love Song'. It is subsequently included on 'Videos' (VVC 144).

SEPTEMBER 17 'This Is Not A Love Song' enters the charts, peaking at number five and remaining in the charts for 10 weeks.

SEPTEMBER 26 Release of 'Live In Tokyo' (VGD 3508). The album is issued as two 12-inch 45 rpm records (à la 'Metal Box'). The tracks are: I: Annalisa/Religion/Low Life/Solitaire/Flowers Of Romance/II: This Is Not A Love Song/Death Disco/Bad Life/Banging The Door/Under The House.

OCTOBER Virgin Music Videos release the 'PiL Live' video, recorded on the 1 July in Tokyo.

OCTOBER 8 'Live In Tokyo' enters the charts, peaking at number 28 and remaining in the charts for six weeks.

OCTOBER 26 John Lydon gives a press conference at the Royal Lancaster Hotel in Bayswater, London. After the conference he gives a brief interview to breakfast TV channel, *TV-am* for broadcast the following morning.

OCTOBER 28 PiL appear on Channel 4's *The Tube* performing 'Anarchy In The UK', 'Flowers Of Romance' and 'This Is Not A Love Song'. Keyboardist Tom Zvoncheck has now been replaced by Arthur Stead. This version of 'Anarchy In The UK' appears incongruously on a semi-legitimate Sex Pistols album called 'Live Worldwide' on Chaos Records (KOMA 788017), credited to The Pistols.

NOVEMBER 1 *ROCKPALAST*, DER ZECHE, BOCHUM, W. GERMANY. PiL make their first 'in concert' appearance on European TV. An entire one-hour show is devoted to an interview with Lydon intercut with the band performing a 12-song set: Annalisa, Religion, Memories, Flowers Of Romance, Solitaire, Chant, Anarchy In The UK, This Is Not A Love Song, Low Life, Under The House, Bad Life, Public Image.

NOVEMBER 2 BRIGHTON TOP RANK: Public Image, Annalisa, Religion, Low Life, Bad Baby, Memories, Flowers Of Romance, Chant, Anarchy In The UK.

NOVEMBER 3 The UK première of the *Order Of Death* film. POOLE ARTS CENTRE.

NOVEMBER 5 READING UNIVERSITY.

NOVEMBER 6 ST AUSTELL CORNWALL COLISEUM.

NOVEMBER 8 BRISTOL STUDIO: Public Image, Low Life, Annalisa, Religion, Memories, Chant, Solitaire.

NOVEMBER 10 MANCHESTER APOLLO: Public Image, Annalisa, Solitaire, Chant, Religion, Flowers Of Romance, Low Life, Memories, Anarchy In The UK, Attack.

NOVEMBER 11 LIVERPOOL ROYAL COURT: Public Image, Low Life, Annalisa, Religion, Memories, Solitaire, Flowers Of Romance, Anarchy In The UK, Chant, This Is Not A Love Song, Attack.

NOVEMBER 13 BIRMINGHAM ODEON: Public Image, Low Life, Annalisa, Religion, Memories, Death Disco, Flowers Of Romance, Chant, Anarchy In The UK, This Is Not A Love Song, Attack.

NOVEMBER 15 NEWCASTLE CITY HALL.

NOVEMBER 16 GLASGOW LOCARNO: Public Image, Low Life, Annalisa, Religion, Memories, Solitaire, Chant, Anarchy In The UK, This Is Not A Love Song, Flowers Of Romance, Attack.

NOVEMBER 18 LEEDS UNIVERSITY: Public Image, Low Life, Annalisa, Religion, Memories, Solitaire, Banging The Door, Flowers Of Romance, Poptones, Chant, Anarchy In The UK, This Is Not A Love Song, Attack.

NOVEMBER 19 AYLESBURY FRIARS.

NOVEMBER 20 NORWICH, EAST ANGLIA UNIVERSITY.

NOVEMBER 22 HAMMERSMITH PALAIS: Public Image, Low Life, Annalisa, Religion, Careering, Solitaire, Flowers Of Romance, Chant, Anarchy In The UK, This Is Not A Love Song, Attack.

NOVEMBER 25 AMSTERDAM.

NOVEMBER 26 DEINZE.

NOVEMBER 28 PARIS.

NOVEMBER 29 LYON.

DECEMBER 1 DUSSELDORF.

DECEMBER 4 HAMMERSMITH PALAIS: Public Image, Low Life, Annalisa, Religion, Memories, Solitaire, Flowers Of Romance, Chant, Anarchy In The UK, This Is Not A Love Song, Attack.

DECEMBER 5 HAMMERSMITH PALAIS: Public Image, Low Life, Annalisa, Religion, Memories, Mad Max, Solitaire, Flowers Of Romance, Chant, Anarchy In The UK, This Is Not A Love Song, Attack.

DECEMBER 7 NOTTINGHAM ROCK CITY.

DECEMBER 8 LOUGHBOROUGH UNIVERSITY: Public Image, Low Life, Annalisa, Religion, Solitaire, Poptones, Anarchy In The UK, This Is Not A Love Song. This show is issued on a bootleg album called 'No More Limits'.

DECEMBER 9 LANCASTER UNIVERSITY.

DECEMBER 11 BLACKBURN KING GEORGES HALL.

DECEMBER 12 BIRMINGHAM ODEON.

DECEMBER 13 CARDIFF TOP RANK.

1984

WINTER 1984 Lydon and Martin Atkins record the 'This Is What You Want . . .' album plus 'Question Mark' (the B-side of 'Bad Life') in London. The bulk of sessions are at Maison Rouge Studios.

MAY 8 The release of 'Bad Life/'Question Mark' as both 7-inch and 12-inch single (VS 675) and (VS 67512).

MAY 19 'Bad Life' enters the charts, peaking at number 71 and remaining in the charts for two weeks.

JUNE 4 The recording of the video for 'Bad Life'. It is subsequently included on 'Videos' (VVC 144).

JUNE John Lydon is interviewed in Los Angeles by Nicky Horne for Channel 4's *Earsay* programme. The 'Bad Life' video is shown at the end of the programme.

JULY 9 The release of 'This Is What You Want, This Is What You Get' (V 2309), PiL's first studio album in over three years. The tracks are: Bad Life/This Is Not A Love Song/Solitaire/Tie Me To The Lamp-post/The Pardon/Where Are You/1981/The Order Of Death.

JULY 21 'This Is What You Want . . .' enters the charts, peaking at 56 and remaining in the charts for two weeks.

AUGUST The US release of 'Commercial Zone – Limited Edition' (XYZ 007) – the last authentic 'PiL' album. The album is exported worldwide but receives minimal distribution. This was the album recorded prior to Levene's departure in 1982-3 at South Park Studios. The track listing (with alternate titles in brackets) goes: Mad Max (Bad Life)/Love Song/Young Brits (Solitaire)/Bad Night/The Slab (Order Of Death)/Lou Reed Part I/Lou Reed Part II (Where Are You)/Blue Water/Miller High Life.

SEPTEMBER 1 An interview with Keith Levene in *Sounds* publicises the release of 'Commercial Zone'. Levene also mentions two musical projects he is working on, using aliases on both of them: The Ninja and The Nerd respectively. Neither of these projects are realised.

AUTUMN Lydon recruits a new band for the resumption of live shows by 'PiL'. Atkins remains as drummer, and is joined by Jebbin Bruni and Mark Schulz, who both start writing songs with Lydon.

NOVEMBER 16 OLYMPIC AUDITORIUM, LOS ANGELES.

NOVEMBER 17 CALIFORNIA THEATRE, SAN DIEGO: Order Of Death, Bad Life, Solitaire, Low Life, Where Are You, 1981, Religion, Tie Me To The Lamp-post, Annalisa, Bodies, Public Image, Chant, Anarchy In The UK, This Is Not A Love Song.

LATE DECEMBER 1984 TO JANUARY 7 1985 Australian Tour, including shows on Christmas Eve and New Year's Eve.

DECEMBER 20 PIER HOTEL, MELBOURNE: Order Of Death, Bad Life, Solitaire, Low Life, Memories, 1981, Religion, Annalisa, Bodies, Public Image, Tie Me To The Lamp-post, Chant, This Is Not A Love Song.

DECEMBER 21 John Lydon and Martin Atkins are interviewed on *The Roadrunner Punk Show*, a Melbourne radio programme on the 3-PBS-FM station.

DECEMBER 31 The release of a 12-inch single, 'World Destruction' by Time Zone, featuring John Lydon and Afrika Bambaata on vocals.

1985

1985 Lydon contributes lead vocals on The Golden Palomino's 'The Animal Speaks' a track on The Palomino's second album, 'Visions Of Excess'.

JUNE 1 It is announced in the UK music press that Martin Atkins has left PiL to form his own record label and concentrate on his Brian Brain ensemble. Both Bruni and Schulz are also 'dropped' from the band by Lydon around the same time.

AUTUMN Lydon records 'Album' in New York with Bill Laswell producing. The musicians used on the record include Ginger Baker, Shankar, Ryuichi Sakamoto and Steve View.

DECEMBER The US release of The Golden Palominos' 'Visions Of Excess' (CELL 6118), featuring Lydon on 'The Animal Speaks'.

1986

JANUARY 16 Malcolm McLaren agrees to hand over Glitterbest and Matrixbest to the control of Lydon, Steve Jones, Paul Cook and Anne Beverly (the mother of Sid Vicious), after a judge had ruled in favour of The Pistols' legal action against McLaren.

JANUARY 21 The release of 'Single' (VS 841) and '12- inch single' (VS 84112). Both releases feature 'Rise'/'Rise' (remix).

JANUARY 27 The recording of the video for 'Rise'. This is subsequently included on 'Videos' (VVC 144).

FEBRUARY 'PiL' appear on *Top Of The Pops* to promote 'Rise'. The band for this appearance comprises assorted friends and acquaintances of John Lydon.

FEBRUARY 1 'Rise' enters the charts, peaking at number 11 and remaining in the charts for eight weeks.

FEBRUARY 3 The release of 'Album' (V 2366). Tracks are: FFF/ Rise/Fishing/Round/Bags/Home/Ease. The cassette and CD versions are, needless to say, entitled 'Cassette' and 'Compact Disc'.

FEBRUARY A 'media blitz' has interviews with John Lydon appearing in some 10 UK magazines in less than a fortnight.

FEBRUARY 15 'Album' enters the charts, peaking at number 10 and remaining in the charts for six weeks.

APRIL 5 There appears in the UK music press an announcement for the new PiL tour and and a new band line-up consisting of John McGeoch – guitar; Lu Edmunds – guitar/keyboards; Alan Dias – bass; Bruce Smith – drums.

JUNE 16 The recording of the video for 'Home'. This is subsequently included on 'Videos' (VVC 144).

JUNE 21 The release of 'Home'/'Round' as both seven-inch (VS 855) and 12-inch single (VS 85512).

MAY PiL make their first appearance in six years on the BBC's *Whistle Test*. They perform both sides of the new single: 'Home' and 'Round'.

MAY 3 'Home' enters the charts, peaking at 75 and remaining in the charts for one week.

MAY 7 HANLEY VICTORIA HALL.

MAY 8 SHEFFIELD CITY HALL.

MAY 10 NEWCASTLE CITY HALL.

MAY 11 EDINBURGH PLAYHOUSE.

MAY 13 ABERDEEN CAPITOL THEATRE.

MAY 14 GLASGOW BARROWLANDS.

MAY 15 PRESTON GUILDHALL.

MAY 17 MANCHESTER APOLLO.

MAY 18 SCARBOROUGH FUTURIST.

MAY 20 LEICESTER DE MONTFORT HALL.

MAY 21 OXFORD APOLLO: Kashmir, FFF, Annalisa, Fishing, Poptones, Pretty Vacant, Banging The Door, Flowers Of Romance, Bags, Round, Home, Public Image, Rise, Low Life, Time Zone, Ease.

MAY 22 POOLE ARTS CENTRE.

MAY 23 SAINT AUSTELL COLISEUM.

MAY 25 BRISTOL COLSTON HALL.

MAY 26 BIRMINGHAM ODEON: Kashmir, FFF, Low Life, Fishing, Poptones, Pretty Vacant, Banging The Door, Flowers Of Romance, Bags, Round, Home, Public Image, This Is Not A Love Song, Rise, Annalisa.

MAY 27 BRIXTON ACADEMY: Kashmir, FFF, Annalisa, Fishing, Poptones, Pretty Vacant, Banging The Door, Flowers Of Romance, Bags, Round, Home, Public Image, Rise, Low Life.

JUNE TO JULY US Tour

JUNE 12 BEACON THEATRE, NEW YORK.

JULY 2 WARFIELD THEATRE, SAN FRANCISCO.

JULY 5 HOLLYWOOD PALLADIUM, LOS ANGELES.

JULY 7 PACIFIC AMPHITHEATRE, COSTA MESA.

SEPTEMBER European Tour

SEPTEMBER 12 Headlining at a show in Vienna on an island on the Danube, PiL have their guitarist John McGeoch hit by a two-litre bottle of wine. McGeoch requires 40 stitches and the remainder of the European tour is cancelled. According to a press release the whole future of the band is in question.

1987

1987 PiL record their first album with a stable line-up for eight years. Sessions are in England, taking place in Milton Keynes, Croydon and Oxford. During breaks in the sessions Lydon and McGeoch also record an album of new studio versions of old PiL songs, intended to be issued as a budget release called 'Renovations'. However only two songs are later released, 'The Suit' and 'Religion' – both as extra tracks on 12-inch singles.

EARLY AUGUST Tour of Scandinavia

AUGUST Lydon is interviewed on ITV's *Hold Tight* programme. 'Seattle' is also played.

AUGUST 10 The release of seven-inch single, 'Seattle'/'Selfish Rubbish' (VS 988) and 12-inch single 'Seattle'/'Selfish Rubbish'/ 'The Suit' (VS 98812).

AUGUST 22 The UK music press announces PiL's 11-date UK tour for September.

AUGUST 29 'Seattle' enters the charts, peaking at number 27 and remaining in the charts for two weeks.

LATE AUGUST TO EARLY SEPTEMBER PiL play a 10-date tour of Brazil/South America.

EARLY SEPTEMBER Lydon is interviewed for Channel 4's *Network Seven* programme.

EARLY SEPTEMBER HOT POINT FESTIVAL, LAUSANNE, SWITZERLAND.

EARLY SEPTEMBER REGGIO EMILIA, BOLOGNA, ITALY. The set is cut short by fans throwing rocks at the band.

SEPTEMBER 14 The release of 'Happy' (V 2455). The tracks are: Seattle/Rules And Regulations/The Body/Save Me/Hard Times/ Open And Revolving/Angry/Fat Chance Hotel.

SEPTEMBER 16 It is announced that PiL have cancelled all dates up to the 24 September because Alan Dais has sprained his wrist and has been ordered by his doctor not to play for a week.

SEPTEMBER 24 EDINBURGH PLAYHOUSE.

SEPTEMBER 25 MANCHESTER APOLLO.

SEPTEMBER 26 'Happy' enters the charts, peaking at number 34 and remaining in the charts for two weeks.

SEPTEMBER 27 CHIPPENHAM GOLD-DIGGERS.

SEPTEMBER 28 LONDON ASTORIA: Save Me, Rise, Seattle, FFF, Open And Revolving, Low Life, Home, Rules And Regulations, Hard Times, Fat Chance Hotel, World Destruction, Angry, The Body, Round, Public Image, Holidays In The Sun, This Is Not A Love Song, Religion.

SEPTEMBER 29 LONDON ASTORIA.

OCTOBER PiL continue their mainland European tour, though an appearance at the Belgian Futurama Festival is cancelled at the last minute.

OCTOBER 31 The release of seven-inch single 'The Body'/'Angry' (VS 1010) and 12-inch single 'The Body'/'Religion'/'Angry' (VST 1010).

NOVEMBER 2 DUNSTABLE QUEENSWAY HALL.

NOVEMBER Keith Levene finally issues his first post-PiL vinyl, a six-track 12-inch EP called '2011 – Back Too Black'. It is issued on Irridescence Records, 481 Woodland Drive, Sierra Madre, CA 91024. All the tracks are instrumentals.

NOVEMBER to DECEMBER 13-date US Tour supported by The Lime Spiders.

DECEMBER 2 WARFIELD THEATRE, SAN FRANCISCO.

DECEMBER 3 UNIVERSAL AMPHITHEATRE, LOS ANGELES. (Last date of US Tour.)

DECEMBER 8 SHIBUYA-KOKAIDO, TOKYO.

DECEMBER 9 KOSEINENKIN-KAIKAN, OSAKA.

DECEMBER 10 SHIBUYA-KOKAIDO, TOKYO.

1988

APRIL John Lydon and Dennis Morris are the jury one night, reviewing current promo videos on London's late night/early morning TV programme, *Night Network*.

AUGUST 31 John Lydon is the subject of a half-hour profile on BBC-2, entitled *That Was Then . . . This Is Now*.

EARLY SEPTEMBER PiL play a festival in Tallin, Estonia.

SEPTEMBER 17/24 PiL and Big Country's trip to Estonia is the subject of a two-week profile entitled *Rock Around The Eastern Bloc* in *Melody Maker*.

SEPTEMBER US CD specialists Rykodisc issue a three-inch CD of Keith Levene's, entitled 'If Six Was Nine'.

DECEMBER PiL are ensconced in the studio recording the long-awaited follow-up to their 1987 album, 'Happy?' Tracks recorded are: Happy, Disappointed, Warrior, U.S.L.S., Spit, Worry, Brave New World, Just Like A Woman, Same Old Story, Armada.